BURGLARS IN BLUE

ART WINSTANLEY

authorHOUSE®

AuthorHouse™
1663 Liberty Drive, Suite 200
Bloomington, IN 47403
www.authorhouse.com
Phone: 1-800-839-8640

First published by AuthorHouse 2/18/2009

ISBN: 978-1-4389-3069-5 (e)
ISBN: 978-1-4389-3068-8 (sc)
ISBN: 978-1-4389-3067-1 (hc)

Library of Congress Control Number: 2008912149

Printed in the United States of America
Bloomington, Indiana

This book is printed on acid-free paper.

THANK YOU

Thank you to the many acquaintances, friends and family who have encouraged me to write this book. Dredging up memories and regrets from the past has sometimes been difficult. However, writing it all down on these pages has been therapeutic for me. I am grateful.

Most of us deal with struggles and demons in our past. Now that I have opened some dark places in my past and let some light shine in, I have found some inner peace that adds a bit of sparkle to my eyes and spring in my step. I hope I never forget.

PREFACE

During the early 1960's, the Denver Police Department was rocked with a police scandal that was the largest case of police corruption of any law enforcement agency in U.S. history. Out of a total force of 775 officers, 53 were arrested and 45 of those arrested ultimately went to prison.

I was the first Denver police officer arrested and the first to be sentenced to the State Penitentiary in Canon City. Being sent to prison after being a cop is the most terrifying nightmare you can imagine.

After my initial indoctrination and orientation in the "fish tank," I was sent to the general population on a Thursday. I didn't get anything to eat until Sunday, and then a fellow inmate spit in my pan.

Contents

THE BEGINNING

POLICE FORCE

ARREST AND TRIAL

PENITENTIARY

PAROLE AND DIVORCE

BACK TO PRISON

FREEDOM

GETTING IT RIGHT

THE TRUTH

The events described in this book are true. No names were changed to protect the innocent or the guilty.

All of the dates and times are accurate to the best of my ability to remember and to research. All places described herein actually exist, or did at the time I encountered them.

I have been as forthcoming in these writings as possible. No attempt was made to deceive the reader or embellish the facts.

The author

HOPELESS DESPAIR

The slamming of the steel doors seemed to grow louder and louder. The smell in the cell house was a mixture of Pine Sol, cigarette smoke and body odor.

Oh God, what am I going to do? I knew that going to the state penitentiary after being a police officer was going to be bad, but I can not survive much longer.

I laid motionless, flat on my back, on my prison bunk. I pulled the cotton sheet up over my head as if I were hiding and also so that no one could see the tears run down my face. I had a bad headache from not eating. I never would have imagined that I could feel such total despair. I was even more discouraged than I was when I was arrested by my fellow police officers. There was nothing in my mind but hopelessness – overwhelming hopelessness.

Can this really be happening? There are no more chances. I'm all out of options. How can I possibly survive this treatment? Why can't the guards see what is happening to me, or do they just not care? This is not a nightmare. I am really here…And I am alone…

I want to scream out for someone to help me, but the people that would hear my cries are not my friends. I have no friends or allies in here. The guards have no respect for me – only distain. I have disgraced the law enforcement community by robbing the people I had sworn to serve and protect.

Perhaps more than some, I hate to be alone. I've always been a get-along, go-along kind of a guy. Wanting people to like me is one of the reasons I'm in here now.

Maybe I should have accepted the warden's offer to do my time in solitary confinement in the isolation unit; at least I would probably get something to eat. This is unbelievable; no one should have to suffer like this. What am I going to do? I don't want to die. I particularly don't want to die locked up in this miserable hell hole.

I thought back to my childhood. We were poor, but I don't ever remember going to bed hungry.

THE BEGINNING

ACCEPTANCE TO

THE POLICE ACADEMY

Saturday, December 21, 1957, was a cool and pleasant Colorado day. Just before noon the letter that I had been waiting for all week finally arrived. It was the happiest day of my life. I thought I was the luckiest guy in the world. I had been accepted into the Denver Police Academy. As a wise man once said, "Be careful what you wish for!"

Holding my three year old daughter, Joan, in my arms, I danced and whirled all around the house.

"Daddy's going to be a policeman."

"Daddy's going to be a policeman."

"Do you hear me, Sweetheart? Daddy's going to be a policeman."

The acceptance process had taken several weeks. First, there was the application, then a background check, a general knowledge and aptitude test, a physical agility test, and an oral interview. I was one of the top candidates offered a position as a cadet with the department.

The police academy started on Wednesday, January 15, 1958. The academy always started on the 15th day of the month to coincide with the pay period. There were 32 male cadets and no women in my class.

Police academies in the 50's and early 60's were woefully inadequate by today's standards. The psychology of police work was not taught. The skills needed in dealing with people as a police officer were not addressed. This was before the Miranda decision became law. Suspects were not treated with the degree of presumed innocence as they are now. The Denver Police Department, as well as most police departments during this time was reactionary. There was little or no public education on protecting yourself against crime or preventing yourself from becoming a victim. The police department waited until someone called and then responded in a way they deemed appropriate.

Many men have developed maturity by the time they reach their twenties. Many are mature beyond their years. I was not. I was far too immature to be married or to have children and certainly too immature to be a police officer. I knew how to fight and handle a gun; that was all I needed.

In spite of the many steps it took to become a police officer, the screening process for selection to the police academy was inadequate. The training was incomplete. The pay was low, ($393 a month for patrolmen) and the temptations to be dishonest were great. The process was flawed in as much as there were no psychological checks in place that might weed out unstable applicants. Some, including myself, wanted the job because we were insecure, or had a poor self image. I wanted the authority of the uniform and the recognition. I needed to be in control.

After becoming a police officer, I thought I had all the answers. I certainly had an abundance of confidence. I thought that money was the answer to everything. Someone once said that people who think money will do anything will probably do anything for money. During this time in my life, I knew the price of everything, and the value of nothing.

I admired all the policemen. I wanted to be one of them. I wanted the power and the authority they had. To "serve and protect" was not part of my agenda. I wanted to be a policeman for my own entertainment and excitement. I wanted to be a policeman for my own personal and selfish gain. I wanted to be a policeman for all the wrong reasons.

For nearly fifty years, I have been processing my involvement in the Denver police scandal and why I took part in it. For a long time, friends have encouraged me to write a book. I doubt that I could have been objective and honest in my writing before now. I have spent so much time trying to justify my involvement and making excuses for my behavior in what happened.

In gathering material for this book, I have read old newspaper accounts and looked at pictures of the police scandal in the archives of the Denver Public Library. It's one of the hardest things I have every done. I get sick when I realize my mistakes and see the wasted years of my life, knowing how different it could have been. The depression that builds in my chest makes it hard to breathe. I feel like I've been hit in the stomach.

I want to be as candid as possible in writing this book, but as I sit here and type, the bitter memories flood my mind and I want to walk away. How could I have been so mindless? How could I have brought so much heartache and sadness to so many? My regret for not standing tall and having enough backbone to do the right thing will continue to torment me. The parts of my story that cause me the most pain to recall are the most significant and meaningful in helping me to cope with my feelings of remorse.

Now that I'm in my seventies, and look back on my life, I realize that I have been fighting a civil war with myself for as long as I can remember.

As in most cases, those who go to prison bring enormous suffering and hardship upon others who did nothing wrong. The shame and humiliation I thrust upon my wife and children will always torment them and me. I know that I broke my mother's and father's hearts.

I am sure that the police departments of every major city in this country have a few bad apples. During the fifties and sixties, before the screening of police applicants was not as thorough as it is today, police wrongdoing was far more prevalent. Honest officers are reluctant to report fellow policemen. No officer wants to be labeled a "snitch." When incidents of wrongdoing are reported, or come to the attention of command personnel, it is usually handled internally, and the public is none the wiser. However, when police officers cross so far over the line and start breaking into businesses in the cover of darkness and cracking safes, acts of police wrongdoing become a far more serious matter than petty thefts, shoplifting and pilfering.

The sixties and early seventies brought an end to the era of police officers having *carte blanche*. It was before Supreme Court decisions that included Miranda, and rulings that had to do with probable cause and illegal search and seizure. Prior to these rulings, a police officer's testimony was believed in court and his authority was rarely challenged. It was felt these changes were necessary to avoid the misuse of police powers. New rules governing conduct and police authority have led to a more equitable system, but it gives a huge advantage to criminals and somewhat ties the hands of the police officer on the street.

I'm sure there were instances where police officers went a bit over the top in gathering evidence, and in doing so, abused their powers. However, I believe these cases were rare and that the pendulum has swung too far in the direction of protecting the rights of criminals at the expense of justice. Criminals do not play by the rules. There are cases where crucial evidence is destroyed or lost while police officers wait for a search warrant to enter a building where criminals or criminal activity is thought to be. A policeman friend of mine from the "old school" said: "Putting bad guys in jail is not a game, and sportsmanship should not be a requirement."

Prior to making application to the department, I served as an auxiliary police officer for two years. Auxiliary officers wear light blue uniforms and work as volunteers primarily assisting regular officers at special events with crowd control and traffic congestion.

One of the perks of an auxiliary officer was being allowed to call the sergeant at any one of four district stations to make arrangements to ride with police officers during their regular tour of duty. I rode along on Friday and Saturday nights. I knew where the action was. I learned all the radio codes. I could hardly wait for the weekends. I thought I was hot stuff. Riding along with regular officers was real police work, it was fun and exciting. I had great stories to tell my friends.

I soon learned that some of the officers were "dirty." At burglary scenes, I observed officers putting items such as cigarettes and bottles of liquor in their pockets. Sometimes money would disappear from crime scenes or from suspects under arrest for drunkenness or possession. I did not see this as something wrong. I perceived it as one of the benefits of the job.

GROWING UP

I was born in Denver and lived there all my life. As most small children do, I lived in a magically wonderful world of innocence. I would run and play without a care. As a child, I had no idea of the hardship my parents endured trying to make things work out and pay the bills. I thought the clothes I wore were new. I had no idea that someone had them before me. They were new to me.

When I was five, my grandfather died. My mother, father, two brothers, and I moved from the little white house which was little more than a roof over our heads, into my grandma's house. The address was 1380 South Columbine Street. The first vivid memories I can recall as a child were when we moved in to grandma's house. Grandma's name was Teany; she was 70. She was a large woman who wore her hair in a bun in the back of her head. The house seemed very big. There was a wire fence along the back of the yard lined with tall hollyhocks. On the north side of the house was a large bed of cosmos. There were morning glories on the lattice near the front porch that sometimes attracted hummingbirds. The world was right. The sun shined brightly and I didn't know the word "bad."

Grandma had a lot of little sayings, many of which I did not understand until I was much older. I still recall some of them and have been known to use them myself from time to time. A few that I can remember:

"He ain't no kind of cowboy less you seen him in the saddle."

"A farting horse will never tire and a farting man is the one to hire."

"A stiff dick has no conscience whatever." (I didn't get that one until junior high school.)

"Be careful about choosing to live in a community that has an abundance of liquor outlets or churches. They are both indicators of despair."

"There's a lot of people out there walking around just because it's against the law to kill 'em."

"We'll just have to make do."

The Second World War had started and food was scarce. We built some hutches and raised rabbits near the big metal garage in back of the house. My brother Tom was eight years older than I was. He went to live part-time and summers with some family friends we called Aunt Olive and Uncle Mannis in LaJunta, a small town in southeastern Colorado. Olive and Mannis had a farm. Tom was big enough to help with chores. Olive and Mannis had lots of room, and plenty to eat.

It was not until I was in about the sixth grade that I began to notice that some of the other kids had more than I did. Some of the things the other kids had were bigger and newer and they had more. By this time, my brother Tom had gone off to the Navy.

By junior high, I began to realize how dysfunctional and pathetic my family was. We all lived with my father's mother. Although my father was a drunk, he went to work every day at the Post Office. It's a mystery to me how he managed to keep his job as a letter carrier.

Many days he went to work drunk, and he always came home that way. He spent his evenings after work and weekends at the Bonnie Brae Tavern. Sometimes late at night, someone would call from the Bonnie Brae and my mother would wake me to go get my father. At 13, and the oldest son at home, I would ride my bicycle to the tavern, put the bike in the back of our old Chevrolet sedan, and drive my father home. Mother and I would help him into the house. I always hoped the neighbors did not see us helping my drunken father into the house. I would have felt sorry for my mother and felt ashamed for my father.

When my mother was very young, she was crippled by a hip injury and walked with a bad limp; she did not drive. I loved my mother very much. Mom had no voice in our home. My father always had the last word. I don't think she was unhappy. She didn't know anything else. She was raised by an alcoholic father. She married an alcoholic and lived in a home that belonged to her mother-in-law. She cleaned, cooked and sought refuge in her church, which she attended alone.

There is one childhood memory that brings me particular sadness. For several years, starting when I was about eight or nine, my father would tell me to dig a hole. I would go out along the fence near the vacant lot next to our house and dig a hole about one and a half feet deep. Later my mother would get a rabbit from one of our many hutches, carry it to the hole, and cut the rabbit's throat. I would hold the rabbit over the hole by its back legs while she skinned and gutted it. This would be our dinner. I didn't mind my part in this, but I hated that my mother had to participate. I felt it belittled her and I could tell by the look on her face that it was unpleasant for her. I resented my father for drinking up the money we needed to buy food.

During the winter of 1951, late on a very cold day, I was working on a friend's 1937 Ford out behind our house. I was 16 years old and cars had become important to me. Somehow I managed to get my hand caught behind the fan belt while the engine was running and ran my hand through the fan. The accident severely cut my left hand. I wrapped it up in a towel and tried to wake my father who was passed out drunk in his living room chair. I could not wake him. He probably would not have been much help even if I could have aroused him. With the towel dripping blood I ran to a neighbor's house and asked them to take me to our doctor. On the way to the doctor's office, I had tears running down my face. My tears were not so much from the pain of my injuries as they were from the humiliation and embarrassment of not being able to wake my father.

I lost the nail on the middle finger of my left hand. It grew back, but it has never been the same. The finger is a constant reminder of an unpleasant part of my childhood.

My father was a strict disciplinarian; I did nothing without his approval. If he was trying to teach me right from wrong, unfortunately, I didn't get the message. I only learned resentment. Perhaps that's why I wanted to be a policeman. I wanted to be the one in charge. In all the years we lived with my father's mother, I never heard Grandma say a word of reprimand or criticism toward my father, her son.

By the time I got to high school, education was not a priority for me. I did not do well. I didn't like it. I didn't care. I was interested in cars, beer, fighting and girls. I was always in some type of trouble. I was in trouble at school for fighting or I was in trouble at home for ditching school. As soon as I got out of one scrape, I would rush headlong into another mess.

As long as I can remember, I have always taken the easy way out. I knew it was wrong, but lying, stealing and cheating seemed okay for me as long as I didn't get caught. My poor mother was always patching me up. While walking home from high school one afternoon, I got into a confrontation with some guys in a car from a rival high school. After exchanging some words and gestures, they got out and a fight ensued. I guess I got my bell rung pretty good because I had amnesia. A neighborhood friend walked me home. My mother was frantic because I couldn't tell her what had happened. She thought I might have been the victim of a hit and run, which was pretty close to the truth. My amnesia lasted only an hour or two, but I never quite figured out how it was possible that I knew there were such things as brothers and sisters, yet I didn't know if I had any. I knew that people lived in houses on streets with names and numbers, I just didn't know what mine were.

At 17, I was a young boy who could not see beyond my next quest for girls, fights, beer, and cigarettes. I was too young to drink but that did not prevent me from sneaking into the local 3.2 bar or having my 18-year-old buddies buy a six pack.

I took a psychology class in high school, but it was only because my buddies did. I had no interest in learning about how other people think or deal with personal situations. I was going to be a policeman, wear a uniform and a badge, and carry a gun. I would be in command. That's all that was important.

During my senior year in high school I learned that my girl-friend, Eleanor, was pregnant. In those days a girl who got pregnant either got married, or went away to help take care of an ailing relative far, far away. Eleanor and I were married early in 1954. She was smart and had enough credits to graduate from high school. I took a job in a grocery store during the day and went to school at night to earn enough credits to graduate. We rented a small apartment and Eleanor found work as a secretary.

At 19, I was married and had a child on the way. I had no training to be a husband or a father. I found myself in a situation that I was not equipped to handle. Now I was an "adult" with a job and a family. I was supposed to be mature.

OFFICER DOWN

Sunday evening January 12, 1958, just three days before I started the police academy, I was riding as an auxiliary officer at the downtown District One Station with officers Whaley and Weston in car eleven. It was a bitter cold night.

At about seven thirty the police radio began to relay the eerie details of an unfolding story about an off-duty Denver police officer who had been shot while trying to question a robbery suspect in North Denver. As more details became available it was learned that the off-duty Denver patrolman, Donald Seick, was out for a Sunday evening drive with his wife and had stopped at a gas station on North Federal Boulevard in north Denver.

As the off-duty officer pulled into the gas station, he observed a suspicious looking man hurriedly leaving the station while clutching something in one hand and the other hand in his jacket pocket. The suspect was on foot. Officer Seick and his wife followed in their car for one block where the officer stepped out of the car and asked the suspect what he was doing in the filling station. The man replied he was just walking. Officer Seick asked the man to take his hand out of his pocket. As the suspect pulled his hand from his jacket pocket the officer could see he was holding a gun. Officer Seick hollered to his wife to duck and reached for his own weapon. As the officer's wife attempted to exit the car on the opposite side of the two men, a shot rang out.

Mrs. Seick ran around the car to find her husband slumped over in the gutter clutching his chest. The suspect walked over and picked up the officer's gun and pointed it at her. She pleaded with him not to shoot. The gunman calmly turned and walked away as Officer Donald Seick, with a bullet in his heart, died in his wife's arms leaving her a widow and their six children without a father.

Within a few hours, through some fast and diligent police work, and perhaps a bit of luck, it was determined that the gas station had indeed been robbed at gun point and the perpetrator of these crimes was a local fellow known to the police as Donald Zorens. He was identified through mug shots that were on file at police headquarters. By midnight, when the shift was nearly over, there was a stack of pictures in the wagon room, (roll call and briefing area.) along with a description and information sheet about the suspect, Don Zorens.

When something like this happens, the department takes it personally. The mind set is, "You hit one of us; you hit us all." I told both officer Whaley and Weston that I would sure like to find that guy. It was agreed that we would check out a pool car from the police garage at the end of our shift. We were going hunting.

As an auxiliary officer I always chose to ride patrol cars in high crime areas where I knew there would be the most action. Although auxiliary officers were not authorized to carry fire arms, I did carry a gun. If a situation ever came up where I really needed a gun, I didn't want to be without one. I had a model 36 Smith & Wesson 38 special, with a two inch barrel. The cylinder only held five rounds, and was small enough that I could easily conceal it.

Some information had been developed about where the suspect might be hanging out. Officer Whaley checked out an unmarked 1955 Ford police car from the motor pool and our hunting trip began. We checked a number of late night coffee places; we drove most of the main drags; we looked in pool halls and bowling alleys and places where we thought he might be. We did not find the suspect. It was getting late, and both officer Whaley and Weston were ready to go home. I convinced them to drop me off at Greens Drive Inn, a 24-hour restaurant near central downtown Denver where Don Zorens was known to have had a thing for a young lady who worked there. I decided that was my best chance for finding him.

I sat near the back in a booth where I could see the parking area and most of the inside of the restaurant. I kept my overcoat on over my auxiliary police uniform, so that I might look as inconspicuous as possible. At one point two uniformed officers came into the restaurant and looked around. I did not recognize them, and they didn't seem to notice me. I checked my revolver several times to make sure I would be ready when Don Zorens walked in. I wanted to kill Don Zorens in the worst way. I imagined different scenarios in which I might have the chance to kill him. I thought to myself that I would kill him even if I were to find him asleep in his mother's arms. Just think of what all the other police officers would say about me. Killing him would be easy. All I would need to say is that I saw him reach inside his jacket like he was going for a gun. I would tell the investigators that I had no choice. Oh how wonderful it would be, if I could only gun down that son of a bitch.

As I sat there sipping my coffee and watching out the window, I imagined the headlines in the newspapers the next day. "CADET OFFICER KILLS SUSPECT IN COP SHOOTING." Or perhaps, "POLICE RECRUIT AVENGES COP KILLING." I would be an instant hero. I would have my picture on the front page of both the Rocky Mountain News, and the Denver Post. The entire police community would praise my good deed.

My dreams were not to be realized; I did not see Don Zorens. I did not have the opportunity to kill him. Don Zorens was arrested a few days later by Denver detectives. He was tried and convicted for the killing of patrolman Donald Seick, and sentenced to life in prison. Don Zorens however, would play a big part in my life some time later.

POLICE FORCE

POLICE ACADEMY

My police academy class began at 8:00 a.m. Wednesday, January 15, 1958, in a large classroom in the upstairs of the 20th Street recreation center in downtown Denver. I had been there before. The building had an unmistakable smell. The odor was a combination of the chlorine used in the swimming pool and the gym downstairs. I had trained to box in the Golden Gloves program while I was a student at Byers Junior High School. The Golden Glove matches were held at the recreation center. My coach, Dolly McGlone, taught physical education for the Denver Public Schools. He was one of the most dedicated teaches the Denver school system ever had. He taught me how to box. McGlone Elementary School in Denver is named in his honor.

During the six weeks we were in training at the academy, I heard several speakers and took notes about things that someone said were important. I was instructed about proper police procedures and shown the proper method for filling in and filing a number of different official police forms. I made several trips to the police firing range located in the basement of the police building. The range officer helped me familiarize myself in the proper handling of firearms. We were given some first aid training. We received some training in traffic control, but other than films, we had no actual driving instruction.

Although the police academy was fun and I enjoyed it, I felt that I already knew everything I needed to know. I had been around guns all my life. I knew how to shoot. During ROTC in high school I was the best. Furthermore, I had been an auxiliary officer for two years. I had seen it all. I was ready to get out on the streets, to do some real police work and to catch some bad guys and put them in jail.

A few things that seemed a little out of the ordinary started to come to light even before the police academy class had ended. The police department furnished the material for our uniforms. All of the cadets were scheduled for measurements and fittings. The overcoats were done only at one wholesale tailor. The shirts were made only at a specific tailor shop. These were the only suppliers on the approved list. The "approved only list" also carried over to our weapons. Officers bought their own firearms. The range officer had to record the numbers and approve the side arm before you were authorized to carry it. We were told to buy a 38 special Smith & Wesson revolver from a specific supplier. If the weapon was not purchased as directed, it would not be approved by the range officer. One officer in my class was insistent on buying a Colt. The gun was new, but only after considerable hassle was the firearm finally approved. It was my feeling that the department gave in rather than make a big issue of the matter. (Nearly all law enforcement officers now carry automatic hand guns as opposed to revolvers. Automatics carry more rounds. In the fifties, automatics were considered unreliable because they sometimes jammed.)

Some of the cadets suspected that there were some kickbacks going on. There were many tailors in the Denver area. There were many outlets for buying hand guns. The "approved only" lists made us suspect that there might be some force in effect going on behind the scene. I thought it was obvious. It seemed blatant to me that there was some hanky-panky business going on. There were conditions of favoritism very early on, which was not a great morale booster. I became somewhat disillusioned. As an auxiliary policeman, I had seen a few officers with "sticky fingers." However, this was the first indication I remember of thinking the police department itself was not all I thought it should be.

I knew that I wanted to be a policeman because I needed to be in charge. I wanted to be somebody. I could boost my self esteem if I wore a badge and carried a gun. However, another cadet in my police academy class was way over the top when it came to being a policeman. When we were in the academy, Jerome Fried seemed like an OK type guy. Occasionally some of us went out for lunch together. Sometimes we went out after class to drink a beer and to talk about the day. Jerome Fried often went with the rest of the group, and I thought he seemed like a pretty regular fellow.

After we were all fitted for our uniforms, there were two or three days during the last week of the academy where we all wore our full uniform to class. I could never have imagined in my wildest dreams that one person could make such a drastic change in his entire demeanor as Jerome Fried when he put on his uniform. His personality changed completely. His posture was different. His walk was different. His jaw was set firm and he spoke with authority. He was a totally different person. Some of the guys in our class used to joke that they could tell if he was wearing his uniform or not, by talking to him on the phone.

I don't know what happened to Officer Fried or where he went after the police academy. I don't remember seeing him on the street.

PROBATIONARY OFFICER

All new officers were on probation for six months, so after the academy, I still had four and a half months of probation. After graduation, each cadet was given an assignment. Assignments and shifts were changed each month to give the rookies a chance to familiarize themselves with the different working procedures and precincts. The new probationary officers usually worked relief, filling in for regular officers on their days off.

My first assignment was the South Denver District Three station, a quiet precinct. I thought this was more fitting for the old policemen, not me. The next month I was assigned to the traffic bureau. I didn't much care for that either. Issuing traffic citations and doing accident investigations were not exciting enough for me.

Working in the traffic bureau was not without incident, however. I was assigned to work with a veteran officer on the late shift, and I had been warned that this particular officer was a stickler for the rules and not to step out of line. Late one evening we were dispatched to an auto accident involving injury in North Denver. A lady who was injured in the accident had been transported to Denver General Hospital by ambulance. We had to go to the hospital to get additional information to complete the report. When we arrived to interview her, it was discovered that her purse with all of her identification and wallet, had been left in her damaged car. Denver General Hospital was only a mile or two from the city impound lot. The officer told me to drive to the car pound, retrieve the purse, and he would finish the report. I was able to retrieve the purse and started back to the hospital. I felt pretty important driving the patrol car all by myself. I was east bound on a one-way street. Near the alley between two major streets, I saw some feet protruding from a doorway. I couldn't just drive by; I had to stop. I turned on the red light and pulled over to the curb. I found a man passed out drunk in the doorway. He looked to be in his fifties. He was wearing bib overalls and a red bandana around his neck. He looked like a railroad worker. I was able to wake him and ask him where he lived. He indicated that he lived near an intersection that was only a few blocks away.

I loaded him into the police cruiser and drove to that location. When we arrived I asked him which house was his and he pointed to the second house from the corner. I told him that he was lucky this time, but that if he did this again, I was going to put him in jail. He thanked me, and I watched as he staggered up the steps to the porch and into the house. I made a mental note of the address. Of course, I was not going to mention any of this to my partner because we were out of service on the accident. If he knew I was getting involved in some other police work there would be hell to pay. I was proud of myself for having done a good deed, and I would let it go at that.

At about dawn, our shift nearly over, we were headed back downtown to the traffic bureau. I heard the dispatcher call the district car that patrolled the area near Denver General Hospital. The dispatcher told the officer to go to an address, and see a lady about a strange man asleep on her couch. It was the very same address where I had taken the drunken railroad worker. I did not bat an eye. I looked straight ahead and pretended not even to hear the call. Not a word was said.

I was acquainted with the officer who had taken the call, and a few days later ran into him in the wagon room.

I said, "Hey, Jim, you had a strange call the other morning over by the hospital. What was that all about?"

"Man, you wouldn't believe it. A guy who worked for the railroad got drunk and went into the wrong house and was sleeping on a lady's couch."

"I guess that lady will learn to lock her door after this," I said.

"Yeah, but the crazy part was that this guy kept insisting that some cop had taken him to that house." Jim responded.

Again I played dumb, a skill that would serve me well.

A month later I was assigned to work relief at the District Two Station in East Denver. I liked working East Denver. The cops were kept busy, and there was a lot of action. Occasionally, I would be assigned to the far east perimeter car. If there was not enough going on to keep us busy on the street, we played a game called "Who's doing Whom." This involved going out to harass the lovers parked on the hill overlooking Stapleton Airport. We would hang back until we saw a car that seemed to be rocking and then go up and demand the car door be opened and some identification be shown. Of course the sole purpose of this maneuver was designed for our own amusement and to see what we could see, and find out who was doing what to whom. We were at the airport late one evening, when I saw a car that had a lot of motion with steamed up windows. I approached the car and with my flashlight tapped on the driver's side window.

"Police department, open the door," I commanded. There seemed to be a lot of climbing around in the car, but no response to my request. Again I pounded on the glass. "This is the police department, open the door," I shouted. About then I see a hand sliding up the window on the inside. Cupped in the open hand is a Denver police badge. "Hey, man, I'm sorry," I hollered. When I told my partner what happened, he asked, "Did you get the badge number?" "Damn," I said, "I was so flustered, I didn't even think to look."

During the time I worked at the East Denver precinct, I worked with an officer they called "pig fucker." The other officers didn't call him "pig fucker" just as a nickname, he earned it. He was a "chippy chaser," a real womanizer. Every time he saw a girl he put the fuck eye on her. This guy would screw any female he could. He screwed the fat haggle toothed skank heifer that washed dishes on the late shift at the all-night greasy spoon, and then bragged about it. This and several other similar instances earned him his well deserved nickname. Finding women is usually not difficult for policeman if that's what they want. I'm not sure if it's the uniform or the status, but something seems to attract the ladies.

At the end of the month, I was again reassigned, this time to headquarters downtown District One Station. I liked working downtown. It was the center of most of the action and excitement. My first assignment after being transferred downtown to the district one station was foot patrol. I walked a beat on 16th Street which was the major downtown business street. The shift was from six in the evening until two in the morning. I walked the beat alone. I stopped at a police call box at certain corners every hour to make a 'pull' which was a call to the dispatcher. Beat cops were more for show or as deterrents than anything. It made the merchants happy. I enjoyed walking the beat. I was a young officer full of energy and self confidence. In the evening light of all the neon signs, I would often see my reflection in the large plate glass windows of store fronts. My belt and shoes were so highly polished they reflected like patent leather. My brass glistened more than gold. I walked tall and felt proud. I knew I was handsome; I could tell by the way young women looked at me. I had it all; I was on top of the world.

My shift was changed on a regular basis. Rookies were used to fill in wherever needed. One Sunday morning I was assigned to work the scout car (paddy wagon) with another probationary officer. Normally they do not put two rookies together, but working the wagon was a no-brainer. The scout car covered the entire city, but there was not much action on Sunday morning. While driving through a city park near downtown, we met two young ladies and struck up a conversation. During our visit we got a call to pick up a prisoner in lower downtown. We told the girls not to go away and that we would be back soon. Car twelve had arrested a drunken derelict who needed to be transported to the city jail. Normally a prisoner would be transported in the patrol car, but this guy had messed himself and was a dirty mess.

We hurried down to pick up the prisoner so that we could get him to jail and get back to the park. The scout car was a Chevrolet Apache with doors on the back like a bread truck. We loaded the man in the back and started toward the jail. I was driving and I nearly missed the traffic light on the first street. I knew that I would have to hurry if I expected to make the next light a block away where I needed to turn. I must have been going fifty miles per hour when I went around the corner. A few blocks later we hear the radio. "Car twelve to scout car one." I picked up the mike and answered.

"Pull over a minute; we need to talk to you." I stopped the wagon, and car twelve pulled up behind us a moment later. I walked back to the patrol car and said, "What's up?" They had a guy in the back of the patrol car. Officer Charles said. "Do you recognize this guy?" "Sweet Jesus." I said, "Where did you get him?" This guy was all bloody, and his clothes were torn to rags. By now you might have guessed that when I went around the corner, the prisoner fell out. Car twelve was behind us and saw the mishap. I again loaded the man in the back of the paddy wagon, with a stern warning that if he got out again, I would charge him with escape. We proceeded to the city jail. The sheriff's deputy at the jail refused the prisoner because of his injuries. We had to take him to Denver General Hospital to get one of his ears stitched back on. This of course meant that we missed our connection with the girls in the park, but no one ever said anything about this incident, and there were no repercussions.

During my first few months with the Denver Police Department I realized that many of the command personnel, from the chief on down, were Masons. It appeared the police department had an "in crowd" of "good old boys" working together. I decided it would be a good career move. It certainly couldn't hurt to be one of the "good old boys." I found a couple of sponsors and made application to the local blue lodge and became a Mason. I proudly wore a flashy ring with a square and compass. I knew the secret hand shake. I was part of the "in crowd."

REGULAR ASSIGNMENT

Not long after my six-month probation period ended, an opening became available in the downtown District One Station. It was on car eleven--a young gung-ho officer's dream. It was the hot car for the district, covering lower downtown and the skid row area.

I immediately applied. I talked to the captain and the sergeant of the detail. The senior officer of the car was officer Weston, who had been my sponsor when I joined the Masons. The captain and the sergeant were also Masons. You guessed it. I got a permanent assignment to car eleven. Back to the beginning: "Be careful what you wish for."

Officer Wayne K. (Wes) Weston was an excellent policeman. He knew his job and he did it well. He had every attribute of an outstanding officer. Wes was the best. He was a man's man. I was proud to have him as my partner. His previous partner, Officer Bobby Whaley, had been transferred to another precinct. The question I should have been asking myself was why had the department felt the need to break up these two officers? I was so happy for the chance to get this assignment that it never occurred to me to question why Whaley had been transferred. By now, it had become apparent, at least to me, that some of the officers were on the take. The practice of "rolling drunks" or picking up items at a burglary scene was common among many of the policemen.

I don't think I ever decided to be a crooked cop. It was just a natural progression. I mentioned earlier that my family was dysfunctional. My father dealt with me by using his fist. My mother dealt with me by taking me to church and praying for my salvation. In any event, the devil won.

I knew Wes well enough to know he was a "player." This meant if an opportunity presented itself for us to score a little extra cash he would be OK with it. I admired Wes and wanted him to like me. I tried hard to make a good impression. Competing with each other to be the best in everything we did made us both better policemen. We had absolute trust in each another, which is vital for policemen working together.

Although radio calls and our duties as policemen were a priority, we were always on the lookout for the opportunity to pick up a little extra cash. We used to joke with each another about finding a "live one" who was carrying a big wad of cash. He told me about a sheep herder from Wyoming who came to Denver a year or so ago who had his entire season's pay in cash and proceeded to get drunk and celebrate. Wes and the cop he was working with at the time evidently helped themselves to some of the sheep herder's money.

There were a couple of times when we first started working together when we handled a drunk who had passed out with more money in his wallet than he had when he arrived at city jail. We would look at each other when checking a wallet for identification. It was an understanding we had about taking some of the cash without saying a word. We were always careful to share the money equally even if the other one did not see one of us pocket the cash. We always shared. It would have been unthinkable to hold out on your partner.

Wes would occasionally make reference to some break-ins or about a safe that was broken into. Of course I asked questions and was very interested. I wanted to please and was anxious to be one of the "boys." Perhaps Wes was just feeling me out. I was more ready and willing than he knew. It never occurred to me to say, "no," or that I didn't want to hear about it. I was caught up in the camaraderie and excitement. I never stopped to consider any of the moral repercussions. We were, after all, policemen; who is going to catch us?

MY FIRST BURGLARY

One night while we were parked on Larimer Street, Wes pointed to a thrift store across the street. "That place got kicked-in last summer," he said. (This happened before I had been assigned to work with Wes.) "There's a small safe under the front counter." "Do you think they keep much money in there?" I asked. Wes said, "They seem to do a pretty good business, and I think it's all cash." It was a big store that sold used clothing, pre-owned furniture and reconditioned small appliances. They were always busy. "Do you think it's something we should look into a little closer?" I asked. "Yeah, I think it might be worth our while to check it out," he said.

Wes said that he thought the safe could be opened without too much trouble. He thought he could do it easily. We decided that on the following Sunday night after the bars closed, if we were not too busy with police work, we would go in and check it out.

On Sunday night we drove by the police parking lot. Wes got a small canvas bag out of the trunk of his personal car and handed it to me. I unrolled the bag and looked inside. Wes told me not to touch anything in the bag unless I put my gloves on. Inside the bag there was a small crowbar, some assorted long slender steel punches and a sledge hammer with the handle cut short. There was also a large pair of channel locks and a flashlight. It was exciting just peering in the bag at the burglary tools. Wes said that he thought everything we would need was in the bag.

Later that night we stopped in front of the thrift store. The street was pretty much deserted. The front door was recessed back about three feet from the store front, which offered some protection of being observed from down the block. I wanted to do my share in this. I told Wes that I would "pop" the door. I felt that if I were going to be a part of this burglary and attempted safe cracking, I should do something besides sit in the car and act as the lookout. We sat in the police cruiser for a moment.

Wes said, "How does it look?"

"Looks good to me," I said.

"Are you ready for this?" Wes asked.

"Yeah man, let's go for it," I replied.

I took the small crowbar and held it close to my side and walked to the door of the thrift store. I pushed the sharp end of the bar between the door and the jam where the lock was located and began to pry the door open. The adrenalin was pumping. My heart was pounding. I was breathing very hard. My eyes darted around inside the store and out to the street. I was scared. Thoughts were racing in my mind. "What am I doing?" "What if someone is watching?" "Is there someone inside?" "What if I get caught?"

The door popped open and swung wide. I pushed it partially closed and walked back to the patrol car. It had only taken a minute. Wes said, "Way to go, partner." I knew I had done a good job of getting the door open.

"OK," Wes said, "cover my ass, I won't be long." He put the canvas bag under his arm and walked into the store.

I sat in the patrol car in case we got a radio call. Again my heart was pounding. If we got a call, I would go to the door and flash my light to get him out. A million things were once again going through my mind. "What if someone stopped to talk?" "What if another police car came by?" "What was I supposed to do if something went wrong?"

It seemed like forever before Wes came to the door and looked out. It had only been ten or twelve minutes. He walked over the car and got in. "Let's roll," he said. "I think we did good," he added.

I drove down and parked under the old twentieth street viaduct, where I knew there would be no one around. Wes opened the bag and showed me what looked like a lot of money stuffed inside. "Damn," I said "How much is in there?" "Quite a lot," I think. We started to count the cash and to lay it all out in neat little piles. The total was over $400.00, and we hadn't started to count all the change.

I asked Wes what he had to do to get the safe open. He said that it was a Yale box (safe) and that after he knocked the dial off the front, there was a big flat nut behind the dial that held the mechanism in the door. He said he used the channel locks to unscrew the big nut and then used a punch to drive the mechanism inside the safe. He said the handle turned freely then and he just opened the door.

I'm not sure how I felt about all this. My feelings were somewhat mixed but I don't remember having any feelings of guilt. My share was a little over $250.00, which was nearly a month's pay at the time. I think I felt pretty damn slick. I thought I was really something. I was one of the big boys now. Of course everything you do once becomes a bit easier the next time.

We did some outstanding police work. He and I were high on the list in our precinct for good arrests. We had made three felony arrests in one month, which was considered outstanding. We were partners; we were a team. Wes and I had a good relationship. We had a great time working together and we often got together socially with other friends and our wives. There was a lot of drinking both on and off duty. I realize now what an important role liquor played in my life. We never got together for anything unless we had plenty of booze. I was young. I was impetuous and very foolish.

I was living in the moment and was happy with my life. Although I had a wife and three small children, I never considered what the future might hold. It was all about partying, friends and the next big score.

SKID ROW

The bars along the strip (skid row) were very accommodating to the uniformed officers in their area. The bar owners knew that much of the time they were being allowed to operate at the mercy of the cops because of various code violations such as serving people who were under the influence. The bar owners were generous with cigarettes and liquor in exchange for our overlooking their bending the rules. The bar owners also knew that plying the officers in their area with goodies would hopefully result in a quick response in the event they had trouble and needed the police.

Many of the derelicts who lived in the area received checks each month from Social Security, veterans' benefits, the welfare department, etc. Many of these men had no permanent address. A number of the bar owners made "friendly" arrangements with these men to have their checks mailed directly to the bar where the check could be cashed and the recipient was given credit toward a running bar tab. This arrangement lent itself to widespread abuse. A lot of bar owners became very wealthy, padding the tabs and overcharging these individuals month after month while the victims remained ignorant as to what was going on, and had little recourse to do anything if they did know. Occasionally one of these men would complain to me, as one of the district police officers, that he felt he was being cheated. Of course, my loyalty was to the bar owner, where I drank and got cigarettes and ate for free. The most I was willing to do was to advise the victim to have his check mailed somewhere else.

During our off-duty socializing, my partner, Wes, introduced me to a long time friend of his, Gene Haas, who had been a deputy sheriff in Arapahoe County, Colorado, for three or four years. About the time I met Gene, he left the sheriff's department. I don't remember the details of his departure, but I don't think it was voluntary.

Gene was a strong stocky guy with a clever wit and a down-home sense of humor that made him easy to like. We quickly became friends. As it turned out, Gene was the third man when we needed help with a burglary or safe job requiring extra manpower. I soon learned that Gene was an excellent safe cracker. Gene and Wes had worked together on a number of safe jobs long before I came on the scene.

About this time, another incident occurred. After I had been on the job about eight months, on one of my days off, I was shopping with my wife at one of the large department stores in downtown Denver. As we stood at a counter, one of the officers that I had worked with in East Denver stepped off the escalator with his wife. He recognized me immediately.

"Hey Art," he said as he turned to his wife. "Honey, this is Officer Winstanley. I worked with him when he was a rookie."

"Art, this is my wife, Gloria."

It was now my turn to introduce him to my wife and for the life of me, all I can remember is "pig fucker." What am I going to do? I can't turn to my wife and say "Oh, Honey, this is my friend, Officer Pig Fucker." "Gee what a surprise, it's nice to see you," I say, trying to buy a little time to perhaps remember if this guy had a name other than "pig fucker." I can't recall it. Finally, I have to confess. "Gosh, I'm embarrassed. I worked with so many officers when I was a rookie, I can't remember your name." As soon as he told me, I acted as though I knew it all along.

POLICE BRUTALITY

The cry of police brutality was not heard much until the 1960's. The early 60's gave rise to the hippies or the beat generation. Youth became more defiant and were challenging the "establishment." The anti-war sentiment during the Vietnam War resulted in many demonstrations as the country pushed for social change. The police found themselves in the middle of these conflicts and reacted with force rather than diplomacy. The shootings of students at Ohio's Kent State University in May of 1970 gave new birth to the term "police brutality." Prior to this period, the cop on the beat referred to it as "street justice."

The primary duties of a policeman, when an unlawful incident occurs, is to gather evidence, protect the scene, and try to determine the truth in regard to all parties involved. The police officer is not there to judge or punish. However, many of us as policemen of the "old school" in the 50's and 60's did not see it quite like that. We wanted to do it all. If you did something that deserved a good ass kicking, you often got it right then and there. Only then were we sure that punishment was swift and justice had been served.

An example of street justice that I remember well was a case involving a car chase. One night a patrol car radioed a chase. The chase went on for quite a while as other police cars converged to the location. This, of course, endangered everyone involved, and adrenalin was running high. Finally, a call came out from the original chase car, "They just spun out and piled up." Glenn Person, the dispatcher, said, "Do you need an ambulance?" The officer replied, "Not yet."

Back in those days, if you were so disrespectful of the law as to attempt to elude the police, you'd better hope they didn't catch you.

Today's policemen are better trained in anger management. They have skills to defuse ugly situations with diplomacy instead of using a night stick. Besides that, there are so many cameras watching everything in the world today, a police officer dare not use unnecessary force for fear of being captured on film.

LEARNING TO CRACK A SAFE

Our opportunities to be burglars in blue were somewhat limited to the shifts we worked which were rotated on the first day of each month. During the day shift we would visit potential businesses that might be targets for a burglary after dark.

Business owners were open to discussing their security systems with the uniformed officers who might happen in to inquire with such questions as, "Do you have a safe, an alarm system, or watchman?" This type of information was invaluable if these businesses were to become possible targets for robbery during the night at a later date. We would "case" the premises carefully for any unforeseen difficulties we might later encounter. There are only two major types of safes: upright, or box type, and cylinder safes. Usually a cylinder safe, whether it is set in a concrete block or mounted in the floor, has to be drilled. An upright safe is either punched, pried or peeled. Because of their limited size, wall safes are usually not found in businesses. Being able to get a look at what type of safe a business might have was important because there were different tools and techniques required for the different types of safes we cracked.

While working the day shift, my partner Wes and I were having lunch at a little place in lower downtown Denver. This place did a very good lunch business, and it was all cash. We were chatting with the owner when one of us mentioned that it appeared he did not have a safe. The owner said that each night at closing time he locked the days receipts in the paper towel dispenser in the ladies' room. When we got back in the cruiser after lunch, I said, "What could be easier than that?" Wes laughed. We gave it some thought, but the truth is that the owner's money was as safe as if he kept it at Fort Knox. It was untouchable. How many people knew where he kept the money? If someone broke in and pried open the paper towel dispenser in the ladies' room, the owner would certainly have to suspect that we had something to do with it.

As police burglars, we almost never went after anything but cash. An exception might be stealing a new set of tires for your own car. Usually, merchandise left a trail and was too easy to trace back to the store; cash was not. Trying to fence stolen goods brings about too much of a risk in getting caught because of the involvement with other parties.

Sometimes, during the night we would call the business from a nearby phone and let it ring while we hurried to listen at the door for the phone ringing inside. A watchman or a night cleanup person would answer a phone after it rang for a long time. If no one answered the phone, we assumed the premises were unoccupied and we could go in. This was long before answering machines were used.

Our procedure for burglarizing a business would be for one of us to break in while the other monitored the radio. (This was before police hand-held radios were available.) If there were some type of silent alarm, or someone called the police because of noise, the dispatcher would put the call out over the air, and the officer in the car would simply say "We're close; we'll cover." This would give the officer monitoring the radio ample time to notify his partner to get out of the building before any other police units arrived on the scene. If other police were dispatched or decided to cover the call, we were the first on the scene and would say it appeared that someone had broken in, or attempted to break in, but were gone when we arrived.

Occasionally we would do a burglary or safe job with other police officers. If it was a particularly difficult job, or near the dividing line of one precinct to another, we would often need to involve other officers. This was not usually our favorite plan because it meant that the cash had to be divided up among more people.

I can't exactly explain how I knew which policemen were burglars and which were not. I just knew the ones who could be trusted and the ones you didn't ask. Wes had been involved in burglaries with other officers before me, and he would tell me which officers he knew to be burglars and which were not. There were some policemen who did not want to be involved with a break-in, but could be trusted not to say anything if they knew.

During my nearly three years with the Denver Police Department, I was involved in about two dozen burglaries, and participated either directly or indirectly with about a dozen other officers in burglaries or safe jobs. The amount of money stolen was usually a few hundred dollars. There were a couple of safe jobs that I was involved in that netted more, but the amount was never over three thousand dollars.

One safe job was not so profitable. There was a tavern in lower downtown that cashed pay checks for many local businesses. It appeared they were doing well, and we thought there was a good possibility they would have a lot of cash on hand. We stopped by a time or two to visit and check the place out. They had a large Keith cylinder safe set in a big block of concrete in the corner behind the bar. Although it was near the front window, there was a window blind that we could close.

We decided to enlist the help of our friend, Gene Haas, because the safe was one that would need to be drilled, and Gene was the best drill man we knew. Gene Haas used to say, "You can do anything with the right tools." In drilling safes, you need good equipment. Drill bits need to be the best titanium or cobalt bits available. The steel used in making safes is the hardest, cold rolled, case hardened, chromium mother of all steel made.

At about 4:00 one morning, we picked up Gene, and the tools we needed, at a pre-determined location near the bar. We pried open the back door with a wonder bar, and went in and quickly closed the blinds at the front window. It took Gene about twenty minutes to get the safe open. I could hardly believe my eyes. The safe was empty except for a nickel and a quarter. This was ten cents each after a three-way split. The business owner took the money home each night rather than leave it at the bar.

Ironically, a little before 9:00 a.m. in the morning, Wes and I get the call to see the owner about a burglary.

In filling out the offense report I asked the owner, "How much money was in the safe?"

"Fifteen hundred dollars," he said. I nearly soiled my linen.

"Wow, that's quite a lot of cash," I said.

"I never leave more than fifteen hundred in there because that's all I'm insured for," he replied.

Wes and I looked at each other. We both knew he was a lying sack of shit, but we can't say a word. This thirty cent safe job played a very important role in my life later.

Many people would see conflict in being a policeman and a thief at the same time. What was I thinking? How could I justify this?   The mind set I had during this time was that I was untouchable. I began to think I was omnipotent. Who could catch me? I'm the police…

MAJOR SAFE JOBS

The Denver police burglars were responsible for two of the largest safe jobs in the history of the city. I was not involved in either of these safe crackings, but I became aware of the circumstances regarding these burglaries.

The largest, and I think the most interesting, was the safe job at the Safeway store at 2309 South Federal Boulevard in Denver. It took place over the 4th of July weekend, 1960. The total amount of cash stolen was over $30,000. In 1960, $30,000 was a great deal of money. Large grocery stores were not open 24 / 7 then as they often are today.

The safe was a large Diebold or Mosler, I can't recall which. It was at least three feet square and stood about seven feet tall. The walls of the safe were solid steel about an inch and a half thick. The method of cutting the safe open was rather ingenious for the time. The burglars used a common electric circular saw, sometimes called a cross cut or skill saw. They removed the saw blade and the guard and replaced the blade with ten inch industrial carborundum cutting diamond chip blade made for cutting steel. (Several of these expensive carborundum steel cutting blades had been stolen months earlier in the burglary of an industrial supply warehouse in downtown Denver.)

The safe was in an office area that could not be seen readily from the street. The burglars rigged up a tarp to cover the safe area where they were working because of the large shower of sparks the steel cutting blade created. One of the police burglars was kept busy running back and forth from the dairy counter with chocolate milk which was poured over the blade to help keep the saw blade cool during the cutting. I'm not sure if chocolate milk was better than regular milk or just closer. The burglars cut a pie-shaped hole in the side of the safe to gain access. You can open more area with a triangle shaped hole with less cutting than any other shape.

Because the cutting blade is round, the amount of steel cut on the outside is much larger than the area of the cut on the inside. This means that you need to start with a pretty good sized hole on the outside. The real danger in this operation is that once you start the cut you must be very careful not to get the blade in a bind. At 5,000 RPM and with no guard on the saw blade, if the blade got in a hard bind and were to break apart, the flying pieces could be lethal. It took the cop burglars several hours, but they were successful in their attempt. They got away with all the money. The saw man in this job, Officer Keith Hutton, later said, "Other than being splattered with a lot of chocolate milk, we got away clean."

The next largest haul in police safe jobs was the removal of a safe from the Gano-Downs store in 1960. Gano-Downs was a high-end apparel store on 17th Street in downtown Denver. The safe reportedly contained over $22,000. After a tip, the safe was retrieved in October 1961, under thirty-seven feet of water in an abandoned mineshaft eighteen miles northwest of Central City, Colorado.

There are some myths about safe cracking that some people have come to believe from watching old movies. For instance, some folks believe that you can strap a few sticks of dynamite to the front of a safe and blow the door off. That will not work. Besides, when explosives are used, it becomes a federal offense, and you don't need the FBI on your case.

Another method you often see in the movies and on TV is to use a cutting torch to cut open a safe. This also is usually not effective. Besides the fact that oxygen and acetylene tanks are heavy and cumbersome to carry, most safes are reinforced with a combination of material such as concrete with asbestos or plaster which will not conduct heat well and will not burn away. If you did find a small safe on which you could use a cutting torch, the hot metal slag from the torch going into the safe as you cut will burn up all the money inside. I'm not sure it would work, but an old safe cracker once told me that if you use a cutting torch to open a safe, you should first drill a hole in the safe and fill it with water to avoid burning up all the money.

Perhaps this would be an appropriate place to mention something that might sound somewhat like a disclaimer. I don't want to get into too much detail about the methods used in cracking safes because I fear that someone would use the information found in this book to open a safe. I don't want to be responsible for supplying the information needed to perform the dastardly deed.

THE WEDDING

Much of the trouble I managed to find was precipitated by booze. During the short time I had been a policeman, I had already earned a reputation for being involved in some crazy stunts. My loss of inhibitions and much of my courage came from a bottle. My drinking was fun; it made me feel like a big man. It also caused me to take matters less seriously than I should have.

One night while working the late shift, I managed to hurry down to one of the gin joints on the strip and to have a couple of double vodka pick-me-ups in the back room before closing time.

A little later on patrol, I observed a car with Kansas tags parked near the Union Station Depot that looked out of place. I got out to investigate and found a young couple in the car. I'm guessing both kids were about seventeen years old. They told me they were in love and had run away from home in Kansas to get married. The couple said they were reluctant to get a motel room because they were a little short on money and they feared they would be asked questions and would have to show some identification.

I explained that Denver was one of the few places in the United States where the city and county were exactly the same. And, that because of this, police officers had the same power as a Justice of the Peace. I explained to them that for four dollars, two bucks each, I could perform the ceremony and they could be married right then and there. They talked it over and agreed that would be a great idea. I had them both kneel on the curb and reach up to put one hand on my badge. I opened my code book and pretended to read the marriage vows. I had them repeat everything I could remember, "To have and to hold; to love, honor and obey; for richer or poorer; in sickness and in health; forsaking all others for as long as you shall live; till death do you part."

I finally pronounced them man and wife and told the young man to kiss the bride. I told the newlyweds that they could go to police headquarters in five days a get a copy of the license, or if they mailed a stamped self addressed envelope, the license would be mailed to them. I wished them good luck and waved as the happily "married" couple drove away. I don't know if they ever tried to get a copy of their marriage license. I never heard another thing about it. I suspect they never knew their marriage was fraudulent. I have often wondered how many children and grandchildren they must have by now.

Denver is actually one of the few places where the city and the county are one and the same, but police officers do not have the authority to perform marriages.

WATERMELON

The area in Southern Colorado known as the San Luis Valley near the town of Rocky Ford is famous for its melons. Cantaloupe and watermelon grown in that area are widely known as the best.

During the summer months large semi trucks loaded with watermelons would deliver to Denargo Market near the rail yards in lower Denver. Denargo Market was the central hub for produce distribution to nearly all of the major retail stores in Colorado.

Because of the size and weight of these trucks, they were not allowed to use the downtown streets in Denver. However, the truckers could save considerable time and distance if they drove in on Market Street to the 23rd Street Viaduct to access Denargo Market. The truckers knew that Market Street was off limits, but during the very early morning hours when there was little or no traffic they would use this more direct route.

At three or four in the morning when I was working that shift, I would pull the trucks over. The drivers all knew why they were being stopped. As I approached the truck, the drivers would usually say,

"What's the problem, officer?"

"I believe you're overloaded about two melons," I'd say.

"Why, yes, sir, I believe you're right," was the reply.

I thought this was real cute, and I would do this whenever I saw a truck full of watermelons down on Market Street.

One morning, I saw a truck loaded with watermelon making its way down Market Street. I pulled in behind the truck and turned on my red lights. The driver stopped, as I approached the cab, the driver started to get out. We immediately recognized each other. It was the same driver I had pulled over a week before. Without saying anything, he just climbed up the front of the trailer and handed me down a big watermelon. I put it in the patrol car and started back as he handed me down another melon. I returned to the patrol car and the driver got back in his truck and continued on his way. Neither of us spoke a word.

THE ASIA CAFÉ

The Asia Café was a small restaurant between Larimer and Lawrence near the alley on 19th Street in lower downtown Denver. It was one of those little out of the way places that served excellent food. It was owned and operated by an elderly Asian couple who the cops and other patrons affectionately referred to as Mama San and Papa San.

I was fond of them both, and I ate there as often as I could. Papa San liked cigars, and I would procure a couple of cigars from the bars along my beat on Larimer Street to take to Papa San. When it was time to pay for the meal I never knew how much money to leave because there was never any bill. I would hold out money in my hand, and Mama San would pick through and take what she said was enough. It never seemed like very much so I would leave some on the table as a tip.

There was a corner booth in the rear of the restaurant near the kitchen that was reserved for policemen only. There was a rather interesting ritual connected to that booth. A large piece of butcher paper was taped to the wall above the booth. When a policeman who regularly ate in the restaurant had his picture in one of the daily Denver newspapers, it was cut out and taped up on the butcher paper above the booth. This also applied to the plain clothes detectives who ate at the Asia Café if they had their pictures in the paper. Occasionally the picture was related to a reprimand or a misdeed by the policeman. There was never any caption, just the picture. I don't believe that Mama San or Papa San could read English, they just recognized the picture, and cut it out of the paper. At midnight on New Year's Eve, the paper was ripped from the wall and put in the trash. A new clean paper was then taped to the wall to start collecting pictures for the New Year.

I'll never forget one late night just before closing when a man went into the Asia Café and ordered food and then refused to pay. There were no policemen in the restaurant at the time and when Mama San demanded he pay for his meal and tried to detain him, the man hit her, knocking her to the ground. Papa San struggled with the man in the restaurant until someone called the police. I was only about eight or ten blocks away when an urgent call came over the police radio that the owners of the Asia Café were calling for help. By the time I arrived the street was so littered with police vehicles there was literally no place to park. That poor bastard had no clue as to the consequences of refusing to pay at the Asia Café. Every cop in the downtown district took a swing at him. Being put in jail and charged with disturbing the peace was nothing compared to the beating the Denver police put on him that night. I'd be willing to bet that he never went back to the Asia Café.

FIREMAN FIREMAN
SAAAVE MY BABY

Denver Fire House Number 4 served much of downtown and was in our patrol district. During the summer, the firemen would bring their chairs out in front and lean them back against the building so they could sit and talk while watching the world go by. The fire station did not have air conditioning back then, nor did the police cars.

Overcome by my need to torment, when I saw them out in front of the station, I would drive by very slowly, almost to a stop, open the mike on the radio in the police car to the public address mode, and say: "Fireman, fireman saaave my baby." Some days I would repeat this little ritual two or three times.

One very hot day, after this had been going on for several weeks, I drove by to chime my little ditty, when to my surprise, two firemen who had concealed themselves between two parked cars jumped up and stuck a very large fire hose in the open window of the patrol car. One of the other firemen released the clamp on the hose at the hydrant. I thought I was going to drown. In the few seconds that it took me to react and speed away, the car was nearly full of water. At the next corner I had to open the doors to let the water out. My wet wool uniform smelled like a dog. All of the official paper work in the car, my log book, my ticket book, my code book was soaked. They got me good. I really felt foolish.

I was surprised that the radio still worked, but a few minutes later I got a call about a bar fight just three blocks away. When I walked in, everybody was looking at me. I realized that my shoes were making a swishing noise as if I were walking in mud. I was too embarrassed to say anything. I wished I would have been quick enough to say something like, "I just saved a baby from a raging river."

PLAY ME A TUNE

About three o'clock one bitter cold winter morning, a call was aired reporting a silent burglar alarm at the Happy Logan Music Company in downtown Denver. The music store was in car twelve's district, but with silent alarms, police often catch burglars in the act because the burglars don't realize they have tripped an alarm. My partner and I, in car eleven, decided to cover car twelve as backup. There was not much going on at that time in the morning, so car thirteen and the sergeant in cruiser ten also covered the call.

This meant there were six policemen and one sergeant at the scene. It was evident from looking through the windows that someone was, or had been, in the store. Drawers and cabinets were open, paper and other items were scattered around. However, in searching around the building we could find no point of entry.

A representative from the burglar alarm company soon arrived with the keys and opened the front door. All of the policemen went in to search for the bad guy. It was discovered that entry had been made by breaking a hole through the wall from an abandoned building adjacent to the music store. In looking around, we did not find any burglars. The owner, Mr. Logan, had been notified, and was on his way to determine what if anything was missing. While we waited for Mr. Logan to arrive, one of the policemen, who was an accomplished pianist,   entertained the rest of us by playing several tunes.

When Mr. Logan arrived, he asked if anyone had looked in the cellar. We had not seen a door that was built into the floor of the back room that could be lifted up to access a three foot crawl space beneath the building. This area was cold, damp and dark. It was used as storage for boxes and displays that were no longer being used.   Because of the limited space, it was decided that the two youngest officers would go through the cellar to make sure there was no one hiding down there.

A young officer who had been in my academy class and I got the assignment.   Bob and I crawled around the cellar with our guns and flashlights in hand while the others were all gathered around the piano upstairs singing, "You are my Sunshine." Suddenly I heard Bob shout, "Freeze." He had found a man crouched down behind some boxes. I holstered my gun and told Bob to cover me while I patted the man down for weapons. As I reached into the suspect's pocket, BOOM! Bob shot him. It sounded like a cannon. When the gun went off, the music stopped. The bullet only missed me by inches. "Jesus, Bob, why did you do that?" I asked.   "I didn't mean to," Bob answered. Bob was wearing gloves, and in covering the suspect he cocked his revolver and was holding the hammer back with his thumb and somehow not realizing how much pressure he was using on the trigger, or his thumb, the gun discharged. By now all the other officers are standing around the cellar door in the floor hollering,

"What's going on down there?" "We're okay." I shouted.

In less than a minute, we concocted the story that the man charged toward Bob and that he had no choice but to shoot. I will say that I would have shot the guy, but that Bob was in my line of fire. We each grabbed an arm and dragged the wounded man upstairs. We laid the guy out on the floor in the back room. The sergeant ran to his cruiser to call for an ambulance to respond to our location on a gun shot wound.

The man was breathing, and had a good pulse, but seemed to be unconscious. We could not find a bullet hole. Finally one of the officers noticed blood seeping out of the suspect's left shoe. Because of the way he had been crouched down, the bullet had entered behind his left ankle and traveled though his foot and was lodged between his toes. He had passed out either from pain or shock. The ambulance took the suspect to Denver General Hospital, and a hold order was placed on him for burglary and assault on a police officer.

I was concerned about this incident, because I knew when it came time to go to court, there would be some conflicting testimony as to what really happened. I didn't want Bob to get into trouble for shooting the guy by mistake, and I didn't want to get into trouble for helping him cover it up. As it turned out, the suspect had several outstanding warrants for burglary in New York, and was extradited out of our jurisdiction. Later I told Bob not to worry about that guy every coming back to Denver because I think he learned that the cops here shoot first and ask questions later.

EXPANDING OUR HORIZONS

My friendship with Gene Haas flourished. We spent much of our time together. He was a better safe cracker than my partner. However, if Wes and I did a job that did not require help, Gene was left out.

The wives of those of us who were involved in burglaries were aware of our activities. I don't remember exactly how I told my wife, but I had convinced her that almost all of the policemen were doing it. I told her everything I thought she wanted to hear. I told her that we always watched for one another. "Don't worry," I said, "We'll never get caught; we're the cops."

At one point during the time I worked car eleven with Wes, we took some days off together and took our wives to Las Vegas to celebrate with some money we had stolen in a burglary and safe cracking. I think it would have been difficult to hide that kind of activity and the extra cash from our spouses. I don't know how the wives felt about their husbands being police burglars, but they seemed to enjoy having the extra money.

Gene and I toyed with the idea that we might find a score that we thought ripe for the picking and pull a safe job on our own on one of my days off when I was not working. We could operate anywhere we chose, but we would be without a police radio for back up in the event someone called the police, or we tripped an alarm. We checked out several places that we thought might be good candidates where we could crack a safe for a big score.

Operating as a burglar while on duty as a policeman meant that I had to confine my burglary activities to the area within my designated precinct. If an alarm went off, or someone called the police, it would arouse suspicions if I was the first car on the scene of a call that was outside my assigned area.

One night we got pretty well liquored up, packed our tools in his pickup truck and away we went. We robbed a bowling alley just on the edge of town. They had a big upright safe that we knocked the dial off of and punched the stem inside. The door opened right up. It was a piece of cake. We made a pretty good haul, and we replenished our liquor supply from the bar.

Things went pretty well for a while. We would check a place out as best we could and then talk about how we would get in and what day and time would be the best. When we decided the time was right, we would go over our plan while sharing a fifth of whisky. We discussed what we might do in the event we were caught in the act. We both carried a 38 caliber pistol and speculated as to whether we would shoot our way out if we got caught. We didn't want to shoot anyone, but we agreed that we would do what we had to do if we were cornered. Then we would go charging off like gang busters.

Over the next few months, we robbed two restaurants in a suburb just outside Denver that proved to be rather profitable. We drilled the safe in the office of a golf course restaurant and we hauled off a safe from a new car dealership that we broke open in the garage when we got home. The next night we dumped the empty safe in the Platte River.

We rationalized our burglary activities by saying we needed the money to better provide for our families, which was not entirely true. There were other opportunities for police officers to earn extra money working as guards or by doing off duty security work. Cracking a safe was an adrenalin rush. It was an exhilarating high that I needed and enjoyed. I craved the excitement and anticipation just before I got the door of a safe opened.

THE BEGINNING OF THE END

Occasionally my partner, Wes, and I stopped at the Alamo Café which was in our district to have coffee or a sandwich. It was a fairly big place that could seat about fifty customers. They had a safe behind the counter that looked like it might be one we could punch. I mentioned this to Wes a couple of times, but being a bit more cautious than I, or having better sense, he said it would not be worth it because he felt the café wouldn't keep much money in the safe.

In April 1960, I was working the day shift, which allowed Gene Haas and me to be burglars at night. Late one night after several drinks, I convinced Gene that punching the safe at the Alamo coffee shop would be a quick and easy score for a few hundred bucks. We grabbed a six pack and the few tools we needed, and jumped in my car to go knock over the Alamo.

I had a set of valid Nebraska license plates that were registered to a lady who had sold her car to my brother. I used big paper clips to attach these plates over the regular plates of my own 1953 Chevrolet sedan when I used my car during my off-duty escapades. I didn't want my own personal plates to be recognized, if, by chance, someone took down the number or the police spotted it at a burglary scene.

When Gene and I got near downtown I stopped to clip the Nebraska plates on over my regular plates, and then we drove to the alley behind the Alamo. We pried open the back door and looked around to make sure the coast was clear. We made our way cautiously to the front of the café and through the front window, looked up and down the street. It was nearly deserted in lower downtown at that time of night.

I knocked the dial off the safe with a sledge hammer and took a long steel punch to drive the stem that held the dial into the safe through the operating assembly. If this can be done the mechanism that keeps the safe locked is useless, and usually the handle will turn and the door will open. The stem would not punch. It was a tapered stem with a bushing, and as hard as I tried, I could not budge the stem. I was frustrated. I thought it was going to be an easy job. We did not bring the tools that were needed to open a safe that could not be punched. The safe was on wheels and we pushed it to the back room so we could not be seen from the street. Again I tried to punch the stem through. Sweat ran down my brow and into my eyes. "Goddamn it, Gene," I shouted in frustration. "Let's put this son of a bitch in the car and take it home." The safe was two feet by three feet, and weighed about 300 pounds. It was a struggle, but we got the safe loaded in the trunk of the Chevy. It was so big, that more than half of it stuck out. It looked a bit precarious sitting in the trunk.

As I got in the car, I noticed a set of headlights coming down the alley. I hurried out to the street and turned. I watched in the side view mirror as the other car turned directly behind us. "Oh shit, Gene, the cops are right behind us." I exclaimed. "What are we going to do?" Gene said. A million thoughts raced through my mind. I sped up and so did the police car.

I knew I could not outrun them. I also knew that if they radioed in a chase, the area would soon be swarming with cops. I thought if I took some evasive maneuvers the safe might fall out and block their path. I sped up, cutting through a parking lot and over some curb stops and careened into the alley behind the parking lot. The safe fell out. The police car went around it and was again right behind us. I felt I had little choice at this point other than to try to talk my way out.

I stopped the car and ran back to the police car praying that I did not get shot. Two police officers got out of the patrol car with their guns pointed at me. I recognized Bob Green, the driver. He was a neighbor who I sometimes shared a ride with when we worked the same shift. "I really fucked up, Bob, let me go." I pleaded. "Get the hell out of here." Bob hollered. I slammed the trunk lid down and got back in the car and drove away.

The next day when I reported for work, the safe was in the wagon room where the sergeant held roll call. It had been brought there by a tow truck, and was being held as evidence in the burglary of the Alamo café. Seeing the safe sitting there on the floor seemed to hit me in the chest. It took my breath away. No one said much about it, but I had the feeling that some of the other officers thought I might have been involved, or that I knew something about it. There is no accuser like a guilty conscious.

A couple of days later Bob Green came by my house and said he had picked up the Nebraska license plate from the street that fell off of my car when the safe tumbled out. "What should I do with this?" he asked. "Damn, Bob," I said "Get rid of it." Bob wired the Nebraska plate to the rear of his little boy's tricycle. I asked Bob about the other officer who was with him the night they stopped us. I did not know him and was concerned about his reaction. I wondered if he was going to be quiet about letting Gene and me go. His name was John Bates. John had been with the Denver police department for over 20 years. Bob said that he was sure that Officer Bates would not say anything now that it was over.

The safe falling out of the trunk of my car was the beginning of the end of my career as a policeman. One of the first repercussions was the wedge it caused between my partner, Wes, and me. He knew that the incident involved me and Haas. Wes was pissed that we had tried to rip off a place and to bring so much heat to our own precinct while off duty. Wes, obviously wiser than I, was disgusted by the stupid thing I had done. His anger made me realize how destructive my actions had become to our relationship.

We continued as partners and worked together, but our relationship was not the same. Much of the trust and faith we shared was gone. Working together had become awkward. The thrill of the hunt for a place to rob was gone. I had messed in our nest to the point that Wes was not ready or willing to take a chance. We talked about one of us asking for another assignment. However, we agreed that would look bad for both of us. We were afraid the brass would become suspicious and wonder what had gone wrong between the two of us.

Wes and I did no more break-ins together. I did, however, do two burglaries that summer outside of the downtown area with Gene Hass.

Meantime, John Bates was troubled by his involvement in allowing a fellow officer, and another man he did not know, to escape a serious felony charge on that fateful April night when he and his partner, Bob Green, let us get away.

A few days after the incident, Officer Bates turned to a long-time friend, Denver Police Captain Ed McCune. He told him the story of what had happened. Captain McCune, believing that Officer Bates, at age 51, was perhaps under a great deal of stress from working the streets, and being close to retirement, might be delusional and was trying to get an early disability retirement.

I don't know exactly who made the decision, but Officer Bates was given ninety days paid administrative leave and referred to the Police psychiatrist for evaluation. At the end of the ninety day evaluation, the doctor reported that indeed Officer Bates was under a great deal of stress, but that his story about letting the officer go free, after a safe fell from the trunk of the car, was probably true.

After many years of rumors and unsolved burglaries, the police administration felt that they could no longer look the other way. They called Officer Bob Green in and confronted him with the information they had. They told him that they had enough evidence to bring charges against him, and that he could only keep his job if he came clean and admitted to exactly what happened the night he and his partner let me go.

Officer Green pledged his full cooperation and went so far as to go home and retrieve the Nebraska license plate from his son's tricycle and offer it to the brass as evidence in their investigation.

ARREST AND TRIAL

ARRESTED

By August, the weather had turned very hot in Denver. The incident of the safe falling from the trunk four months before had all but been forgotten. At least I thought so. I went about my merry way as though the world was mine to do with as I pleased.

On Wednesday, August 3, 1960, my family and some friends went water skiing.

Late in the afternoon, when I pulled up in front of my home, towing my boat with my family in the car, I saw an unmarked police car with two detectives parked across the street. My heart was in my throat as the detectives left their car and walked toward me. I invited them into the house. I wanted to appear as nonchalant and innocent as possible, but deep in my heart, I think I knew this was the worst thing in the world.

One of the detectives said "Art, the Chief wants to talk to you."

"About what?" I inquired.

"We don't know," He said, "He just asked us to bring you into headquarters."

"Am I under arrest?" I asked

"Yes," one of the detectives said. "You'll need to bring your badge and police ID card."

I was in a daze; how could this be happening to me? It was like a bad dream. I turned to my wife and told her not to worry. We would get everything straightened out and that I would be home soon. The detectives demonstrated the professional courtesy of not putting me in handcuffs in front of my family.

On the third floor of the police building, in the Chief's office, I surrendered my badge and official police identification. I was informed that I was suspended as a police officer and being charged with the burglary of the Alamo Café. Division Chief Walter Nelson asked me if I wanted to make a statement. "I have nothing to say about this," I stated. "You guys have got some bad information; I had nothing to do with any of this." A few minutes later, I was on the top floor of the police building in the city jail. I was wearing my under shorts and a pair of coveralls that were too big. It was noisy and the steel and concrete of my jail cell seemed very cold.

It all seemed like a blur. I believed that I would be able to talk my way out of this mess just as I had done all my life. I was somehow convinced that the authorities would believe a nice young man like me over anyone else. I spent the next two days being taken down to the detective bureau every few hours for interrogation. I maintained my innocence. I told them they were nuts and that I had nothing to do with this or any other type of wrongdoing.

On the third day, my wife's family arranged bail and I was released to go home. By now the newspapers were full of speculation about me as a police officer being questioned about alleged break-ins and how widespread the corruption might be. The Chief of Police and the district attorney assured the media that this was an isolated incident of possible wrongdoing that they were looking into. They told the press that it was just one case of a cop possibly gone wrong. Other than that, they had no comment.

I was able to retain two lawyers who told me they could offer the best defense possible. "Let us handle this for you, and everything will turn out just fine," they assured me. Even this early on, the police scandal was a high profile case, and was generating a lot of media coverage. It was a great opportunity for a couple of attorneys to garner attention and to be recognized.

As the police administration tried their best to make it all sound as if it were a minor case of police wrongdoing, the Denver newspapers pushed harder and dug deeper. Both The Denver Post and the Rocky Mountain News hammered away at the rumors of widespread police corruption. One veteran police reporter in particular, Al Nakkula of the Rocky Mountain News was persistent in his beliefs that the scandal went much deeper. Amid threats from his editor and long time friends in the police department to back off, he continued to pursue the issue. He challenged the police department to explain why a major burglary or safe cracking in the metro area had not been solved in over two years. Although it nearly cost him his job and many friends, Al Nakkula was eventually given credit for bringing to light the full story of the Denver police scandal. However, he was not alone in his determination to get to the bottom of police corruption. Zeke Scher, who was the court reporter for the Denver Post, was relentless in his search to uncover the truth. In his stubborn refusal to let the story die he brought light to the police scandal for all to see. A lot of people hated Zeke Scher for reporting the truth.

The history of a free press and investigative reporting in this country has proven many times that it is one of the most powerful tools we have to assure and protect our freedoms.

I realize now that my thinking process or rationale during this period of my life was seriously flawed. Most of the choices I had made since high school were wrong. I'd like to have benefit of the insight I have now and go back to about the time I started to grow pubic hair and have another shot at the world.

When I chose to become a burglar with the other policemen, I thought I was joining a group of real tight friends. I thought of it as an elite group of guys that shared a special bond. After my release from jail on bond I continued to maintain my innocence. I found some menial jobs to help with the bills, but it was hardly enough. My attorneys and the cost of my up-coming defense were going to be expensive. I was naïve to think that all the policemen that I called "friends" would come to my aid. I was protecting many police officers in matters of wrongdoing by keeping my mouth shut. I expected them to rally behind me with a huge outpouring of support. Just the opposite turned out to be the case. They avoided me like the plague. They acted as though I did not exist. My policemen "friends" were so paranoid that they were being watched or that their phones were tapped they pretended not to know me. I felt abandoned and alone. Other than my family, I had no one to talk with or turn to. My "friends" and associates were all gone.

TRIAL

In October, 1960, just two months after my arrest, I went on trial for the burglary and theft of the safe from the Alamo Coffee Shop. The prosecution had strong evidence. The testimony of both policemen John Bates and Bob Green who had stopped me and then let me go was damaging. The testimony of the lady who had sold my brother the car with the Nebraska license plate that was recovered by the police was also very incriminating.

When the jury returned after their deliberation they filed back into the court room without looking at me or even looking my way. That is not a good sign.

After a week of testimony and one day of jury deliberation, the jury found me guilty of receiving stolen property and conspiracy, but not guilty of burglary, larceny and conspiracy to commit each. The verdict was confusing. Why the conviction of receiving stolen property and conspiracy and not burglary? Did the jury think someone else stole the safe and then loaded it in my car? My attorneys seem to think the jury felt I was somewhat guilty in all of this but perhaps not entirely to blame.

My attorneys again assured me that they could win the case on appeal and the guilty verdict would be overturned. A defendant often has an advantage in an appeal because the prosecution has shown its hand. You know what evidence they have and can better prepare to defend yourself against it. We immediately filed an appeal for a new trial, and my bond was continued. I have long since learned that as long as a defendant has the money to pay for it, there is an attorney willing to file an appeal.

I continued to believe that I would be exonerated. I believed I would be a policeman again. I believed it because I wanted it so much.

For the next two months I worked at different construction jobs during the day and drove a cab at night. The bills continued to pile up. Taking care of my family and making payment to the lawyers were taking a toll.

ARRESTED AGAIN

I thought that money would fix anything. All I needed to do was to find a way to come up with enough money to pay the attorneys and let them know that I had sufficient funds to fight these charges, and that it would all go away.

Driving a cab at night gave me the opportunity to look for a place to rob. It would have to be a special score. The circumstances would have to be just right. It would have to be a job that I could do alone. I would not have the back up of a police radio to alert me to an alarm. It would be risky, but I was desperate. (The line between desperation and desperado is very thin.)

I found the place. It was the Super Drug in South Denver. I checked it out carefully. There was no alarm system. There was a safe I could punch and there was probably a good bit of cash. All I would need would be a good alloy tapered punch and a small sledge hammer with a short handle.

Normally the drugstore was open late, but on Christmas night, they closed early. I was ready. There would not be much traffic. I parked my cab in the lot of a nearby all-night restaurant. I called the Super Drug from a nearby pay phone and left the receiver off the hook. I walked over to the store and listened at the door. I could hear the phone ringing inside. I went back to the pay phone and hung up the receiver. I thought to myself, "So far so good." I went to the back of the store and pried open the back door. Once the door was open, I banged on it loudly and shouted, "Hey, what the hell is going on in here." I then walked away and stood in the shadows at the rear of another business about a half a block away where I could see the back of the drugstore. I waited to make sure that no one came and the police did not respond to some type of alarm that I might have missed. After fifteen or twenty minutes I decided it was safe to go in and punch the safe. In the dim light of the back room, the safe looked tempting and exciting. I knocked the dial off and punched the stem inside the safe. I had the door open in just a few minutes. In the office near the safe, I found a large pink wastebasket that I grabbed and started to fill with money from the safe. My heart was beating very fast; there was a lot of money. I needed to get it all in the wastebasket and get the hell out of there.

As calmly and nonchalant as I could, I walked out of the back door carrying the pink wastebasket full of money. I crossed the parking lot and walked the short distance to the restaurant where the cab was parked. I put the wastebasket on the floor in the front seat of the taxi. I put the punch and the hammer on top of the money and covered it all with my jacket.

I had pulled it off beautifully. I was home free. The adrenalin rush was still there. It was a perfect score. I had gotten away clean, I was excited. I felt proud and wished I could have shared the moment with someone else.

I drove around basking in the feeling that things were going to be better now. The immediate pressure was off and the money would provide a solution to most of my problems for the time being.

The taxi business was slow. I informed the dispatcher that I had picked up a fare. I did not want to be called, and now I could afford to pay the rent on the cab. I just needed to drive around a while until it was near the end of my shift; then I would put the wastebasket in my own car in the parking lot of the cab company and turn in my cab as usual.

I drove to Aurora, a suburb just east of Denver. I was stopped for a light at a major intersection. An Aurora police cruiser pulled up next to me and the officers in the police car recognized me. My picture had been in the newspapers and on television so much the past few months they knew who I was. The officers were curious as to why I was there or what I was doing and decided to stop me. After the light changed, they pulled in behind me and turned on their red lights. I stopped the cab and walked back to the police car. As I talked to the driver, the other officer got out and went up to the cab. A moment later I heard the other officer say, "Put your hands up." I turned to see him pointing his gun at me. He had found the wastebasket full of money and the burglary tools in the front of the taxi. This could not happen today as property cannot be searched without probable cause. I panicked. I shouted, "Do you know who I am?" How stupid. Of course they knew who I was; that's why they stopped me. I felt as though the life was draining out of me. I offered the officers all the money if they would just let me go. Not a cool move to two policemen who thought their only job was to uphold the law. As if things were not bad enough, they found a loaded 25 caliber Browning automatic pistol under the front seat. It had been my back-up gun when I was a cop. I carried it in a leg holster under my uniform pants. I carried the gun in the cab in case I was robbed or found a need to protect myself.

I was handcuffed and transported to the Aurora City jail. The next morning, two Denver Police detectives came and took me back to police headquarters in Denver. By now they had put two and two together, and knew I had robbed the Super Drug in South Denver. The interrogation seemed endless. I was taken downstairs from the city jail every two or three hours day and night. I insisted they were wrong, and that I had found the wastebasket full of money. I was only trying to fool myself. The near constant interrogation was wearing on me. I could not get enough sleep to feel anything but tired. I dreaded lying down to sleep. I wished there was a way to make the nightmares stop.

Fifty years later, as I write this, it is difficult for me to imagine how screwed up my thinking was. How dare I think that this might all go away? What right did I have to think I could be a policeman again? How could I imagine that stealing more money would get me out of a situation caused by stealing money? The horror of it all is clear as if it happened yesterday. I was so naive, so selfish, and so stupid.

THE MOMENT OF TRUTH

By the end of December, I had been in jail for 5 days. It was around two in the morning. I woke up crying. This was not a bad dream; it was real. I was in the Denver City jail. Reality hit me. The moment of truth had finally arrived. I sobbed to myself, "What have I done?" The only job I ever wanted was gone. My dream of being a policeman had come true and I let it slip through my fingers. All I had hoped for was destroyed. How could this be happening? How could I ever find a job after what I had done? I have ruined everything. The other policemen are not going to help me. My police department was now against me. "Oh, God," I cried, "I'm alone; what will I do?"

As I lay on my bunk, the feelings of shame and pity were overwhelming. Had I really done this myself? It seemed so unfair. Why had someone not warned me?

Tears ran down my cheeks. I shivered from the cold. I did not move in my bunk for a long time. I felt so ashamed. I had brought disgrace to my mother and father, my brothers, and my friends. I had disgraced my wife and children. I had disgraced the job and myself. How will I ever be able to hold my head up and walk tall again?

I decided that my best shot was to cooperate to the extent of at least confessing to the burglaries I was involved in and try to cut some kind of a deal to get out of the mess.

The next day when my wife Eleanor came to visit, I told her I could no longer carry the heat alone. I told her to call my partner Wes, and to get word to Gene Haas to clean up anything they had that would incriminate themselves. I told her that I was going to confess. I had already admitted my involvement without knowing it during previous visits with my wife. In the city jail, the inmate visiting booth was bugged. Inmates communicated with visitors by a phone and could see each other through a thick glass partition. The conversations were recorded. I was so naïve. Even after being a police officer, I did not snap to the fact that the intelligence bureau had wired into the system and could listen and record any conversation they felt they needed to. The information they gleaned from listening to inmates' conversations could not be used in court as evidence, because it was gathered illegally and they did not want this practice of listening to private conversations to be known. It was, however, considered a smart move, and a wonderful tool in helping to solve crime. Today that would be a real "no-no."

On New Year's Eve, I informed the chief of detectives, Division Chief Walter Nelson, that I was willing to talk about the burglaries, but only the ones that I was personally involved in—nothing else.

A meeting was hastily called involving The Chief of Police James Childers, District Attorney Bert Keating, Division Chief Walt Nelson and Detective Captain Jack Haeflinger.

CHERRY PIE

When the brass was all assembled on the third floor in Detective Chief Walt Nelson's office, I was brought down from my jail cell which was on the top floor of the police building. Somehow what was going on had leaked to the media, and the third floor was swarming with people from the press and the news media. I suspect they were alerted when District Attorney Burt Keating and Chief of Police Jim Childers showed up at police headquarters on New Year's Eve!

Detective Captain Jack Haeflinger had a stack of all the offence reports involving burglaries over the past year or two. There were more than a hundred. I started looking through the burglary reports, setting aside the ones that I had done. There were many reports that I knew police officers were responsible for--perhaps twenty or thirty, but if I had not been involved, I said nothing and passed them by with no comment. By the time I had reached the bottom of the pile, I had set aside more than a dozen reports. I told them these were burglaries I had committed and had first hand knowledge of. I would not discuss any other suspected burglaries where they thought police officers might be involved. By the time I had finished, I had been in the office about two hours. To avoid the media people who were gathered outside the detective bureau, I was escorted out a side door that led into the auto theft bureau and taken down the hall to an elevator to be sent back to my jail cell upstairs.

The Chief of Police and the District Attorney were now going to have to face the people from the media gathered outside the office with an explanation of what was going on. They would have to admit that the suspected police corruption was indeed larger than they had first reported. While planning their strategy as to what a press release should say, they sent out for some coffee and refreshments. A short time later a uniformed officer by the name of Mackey walked into the detective bureau carrying a large carafe of coffee and a cherry pie.

The Sunday morning newspapers of January 1, 1961, awakened Denver with these headlines:

WINSTANLEY CRACKS FOR CHERRY PIE
BIG BREAK LOOMS IN POLICE PROBE
WINSTANLEY FAMILY UNDER SPECIAL GUARD

I was not aware of this story being carried in the newspapers for several days. I never saw the cherry pie. I was back in my cell in the city jail when the pie was delivered. However, the rumor of my confessing for a cherry pie followed me for years.

As a result of my spilling my guts for a "piece of cherry pie," during the next four or five days, five Denver policemen were suspended and jailed for investigation of burglaries.

I remained in jail. I was deemed a threat to society, and my bond was substantially increased.

The emotions of the people of Denver and the surrounding communities ranged from outrage to disbelief. But as the man with the big hat in the circus says, "The show is just beginning; you ain't seen nothing yet."

SENTENCING

The turn of events since my admitting to the burglaries and safe jobs I was involved in brought about some changes. Although District Attorney Burt Keating said my cooperation was only limited, he did cut me a little slack. The amount of my bond was somewhat reduced, and I was able to get out of jail by mid January. I withdrew my appeal on the charges I was convicted of, with the understanding that no new charges would be filed against me as a result of my implicating myself in other burglaries.

I remained out of jail on bond for about six weeks until it was time for me to return to court. My sentencing date on the conspiracy and receiving charges was Tuesday, February 28. 1961. My wife drove me to the Denver City and County Building. I walked up to the district courtroom where I had been convicted. I was to be sentenced by Judge Don Bowman, who had been the trial judge. Down deep in my gut I think I knew that I was not going to get probation, but I did not think I would be sentenced to jail for more than a year or two at the most.

I sat on the bench near the front of the courtroom with my wife and my attorney awaiting my turn. The judge was taking care of some other court business. I felt very heavy. My breathing became labored. Everything seemed to be going in slow motion. When I heard my name called out, I stood and started toward the front of the courtroom. I felt numb. Things did not seem real. I felt as though I was off in the distance watching the proceedings from afar. All I remember hearing was the judge saying 4 to 8 years in the state penitentiary. Then I heard myself say, "Oh, Your Honor, I can't do that much time." Judge Bowman leaned forward from the bench and said, "Well, son, you go do what you can of it." I was in a state of shock. Four to eight years seemed like a lifetime. I would never survive. How could I ever do that much time?

I was remanded to the Sheriff's department. Two uniformed sheriff officers escorted me to a holding cell in the City and County building. From there I was transported to the Denver County jail to await the "pulling of the chain." The expression "pulling of the chain" was jail house talk for the day when there were enough convicted prisoners to make it worth the trip to put them all on a bus and transport them to the State Penitentiary at Canon City. The prison is about a hundred and ten miles south of Denver.

At about eight in the morning on Friday, March 3, 1961, I heard one of the sheriffs holler, "Winstanley, wrap it up." I was not sure what was going on at the time, but I soon learned that "wrap it up," is jail talk for get your stuff together, you're being moved. I guess the sheriff's department thought I was someone special or that I was a security risk because I was not going to be transported to prison on the bus with the other sentenced prisoners. I was being taken alone in a sheriff's car by two deputies.

I was handcuffed to a chain around my waist and shackled at the ankles. The car I rode in was a light green 1959 Plymouth Fury. It had rained some the night before, and as we traveled, occasionally I could hear a splashing when the car hit a wet spot in the road. I don't think I thought of suicide as an answer, but I wished the car would somehow go out of control and I would be killed. I knew that I would not survive being in prison. I had an overwhelming desire to say something to my children. My three children, Joan, 6, Diane, 4, and Mike, 2, were suddenly more important than anything else. I felt there had to be some words that I could leave them that they could hold onto--words to carry them through life that would somehow keep them safe forever. Some words that would assure them how much I loved them. The words never came.

PENITENTIARY

THE FISH TANK

I arrived at the penitentiary about noon on Friday, March 3, 1961. A lot of things happened rather quickly, and my first few days were somewhat of a blur. The first thing that I remember happening was being told to strip naked and told to take a long hot shower while being watched by a prison guard. I was then given a very thorough cavity search and my head was shaved. I was given some prison clothes and marched off to the infirmary where two or three inmate nurses took blood samples and checked my body from top to "bottom." They even looked in my mouth and checked my teeth.

I was in the "fish tank." All new arrivals spend their first three or four weeks in cell house four. New arrivals are called "fish." Cell house four is the fish tank. I'm not sure where the term "fish" originated, but new inmates are called "fish" in every jail that I ever heard of. I also happen to know that a new unsuspecting player in a poker game is called a "fish."

I believe a novice or beginner in many things is often referred to as a "fish."

The three or four weeks a new inmate was in the fish tank were for indoctrination and evaluation. We were given tests for everything from reading to aptitude and there were also tests for social and behavior skills. We were given chest x-rays and checked for everything from hearing loss to color blindness. I was in the fish tank long enough to know that an inmate who claims not to have pulled his wool blanket over his head at night and cried is a liar.

Each afternoon we had instruction from someone from the prison staff about the "do's" and "don'ts" of the institution. The list of rules seemed endless. You could lose your privileges and even be sent to the "hole" for whistling. Inmates can use whistling to signal one another, and of course any type of signaling and signing is not allowed.

After a few days, cell house four seemed to have a rather secure feeling about it. The routine seemed to offer some comfort. Cell house four had some history. It was the only building still standing from the days when it was a territorial prison before Colorado became a state in 1876. It was a square two story building made of stone that was quarried from the hard rock mines of the Canon City area in the eighteen hundreds.

The fish tank was very clean and smelled fresh. We wiped the walls down and mopped the floors every morning before breakfast. The cleaning solution and mop water we used contained some type of disinfectant that made the cell house and our hands smell like Lysol. The concrete floor of the walkways was worn concave from foot traffic, and there was a noticeable dip in the floor in front of each heavy steel cell door. There were less than twenty men in the cell house, all of whom seemed just as frightened as I was. Each day one or two would leave for the general population, and we would get one or two new convicts. We were taken to the chow hall for our meals at times when we were the only ones there. During our time in the fish tank, there was no contact with the general population. Cell house four was quiet and orderly and at times I felt peaceful.

However, the anxiety and fear grew each day as the time got closer to being sent from cell house four to the general population. After being a policeman, that day was more terrifying to me than most. I could only imagine how inmates felt about ex-cops.

The day before I was scheduled to be released into the general population, a guard was sent to escort me to the main administration building. I was taken to Warden Harry Tinsley's office. The guard and I waited in the outer office for a few minutes. I knew something was up. This was not the way it usually worked. Something different was about to take place. The door opened, and I was asked to come in. When I entered, Warden Tinsley introduced himself to me and we shook hands. He also introduced me to the other two men that were seated in the office. They were Assistant Warden Fred Wise and the Director of Security Captain Yoe. The warden introduced me by my name. It was the first time in weeks I had been referred to as anyone other than 33123.

Warden Tinsley said, "We have something to discuss with you, and we want you to give it careful consideration." A million thoughts raced through my mind.

He said, "Your safety is our main concern and we would like you to consider doing your time in cell house three."

Wow, by now, I had heard about cell house three. That was the isolation block. That's where death row was.

"What does that mean?" I asked.

Captain Yoe responded, "We feel that you would not be safe out in the population, and it is impossible for us to assure that you will not be hurt."

Associate Warden Fred Wise said, "You would be safe in cell house three; you would be more or less isolated from the other inmates."

"Are you asking me to do my entire sentence in isolation?" I asked.

Warden Tinsley said, "That's what we feel would be best for everyone."

I thought about it long and hard for about one minute and said, "No."

I had resigned myself to the fact that I was probably not going to survive this ordeal, but doing four to eight years in isolation would be worse than death.

Warden Tinsley said, "We can not force you into isolation, but if you enter the population tomorrow you are going to have a tough time. You have no friends in here."

"Do you understand what we are saying?" asked Captain Yoe.

"Yes, sir, I understand," I replied.

"Well, if that's your decision, then it's your decision," the warden said.

"You had best avoid going to the yard and to the movies on Sunday," he added.

Captain Yoe said, "If you change your mind, get word to one of us."

"Thank you, sir," I said.

As we stood and shook hands one of them said, "Good luck, Art."

GENERAL POPULATION

At 10:00 a.m. Thursday, March 30, 1961, the day after meeting with the warden, I was moved to "general population." I was assigned to cell house six, 2–2 R. That was the second cell on the second tier of the right bank. It was not a mistake that my cell assignment was the second cell from the front of the cell house. The cage (guard station) was at the front of the cell house and the administration felt I would be safer near the cage. The guards could also respond quicker in case of trouble.

The cell was tiny. It was about six by eight feet. The walls and ceiling were painted a light shade of green. There was a two inch thick canvas covered mattress, two worn bed sheets and a dark gray wool army blanket on the iron bunk that was welded in place. On the floor was a half roll of toilet paper next to a cast iron toilet. The toilet had no lid or seat.

The prison grapevine is an amazing network of information that travels with remarkable speed. The entire population was aware of my presence at the prison and knew who I was from the moment I first arrived at the fish tank. Of course everyone knew I was being assigned to cell house six before I arrived.

Many of the inmates had small mirrors they would hold outside the bars so they could see down the tier. They wanted to get a glimpse of who was coming and going. Sometimes they would use the mirrors to flash signals to one another. Holding a mirror out of your cell was against the rules, and the guards would take them if you were caught, but the inmates would usually have another one in a few days.

I was scared. I thought I was going to be sick. I could feel the tension in the air. It was frightening to know that the other inmates were watching my every move. I sat in my cell until the horn sounded for lunch, and all the doors opened. I stepped out of my cell and waited on the tier with all the other inmates until the all clear bell sounded and the doors were closed. We all started to file into a line to go to the chow hall. Talking was not allowed. There was a very fat guard that walked along the line while we marched off to chow. If anyone spoke, he would holler, "Dummy up!"

Long lines from the other cell houses all converged on the chow hall which was a large building in the center of the prison complex. As we walked in we picked up a steel compartmented tray and a large spoon. The tablespoon was the only utensil. Lines of inmates came from both sides and converged at a large double row of steam tables that served food from both sides cafeteria style and split at the center where the inmates walked to their seat. Guards directed every other inmate to a different side of the chow hall as they came off the line. This was done to prevent buddies or friends from sitting together and cooking something up on their own. You never had the same man on either side of you in the chow hall. The chow hall was filled from the back to the front in a very orderly fashion. We ate at long steel tables and sat on steel benches, all of which were bolted and welded to the concrete floor.

I moved through the chow line like everyone else with one exception. The food was dished up by inmates who worked in the kitchen. They would not put any food in my pan. The line continued to move. I was ignored as if I were invisible. You could not stop or hold up the line.

The evening meal was no different. I was again invisible. I could not talk to a guard. Inmates did not talk to guards. If you needed to talk to someone in the administration or see a doctor, or see anyone about anything, the procedure was to go to the cell house clerk who was an inmate and get the proper request form. If an inmate was observed talking with a guard, he was automatically labeled a "snitch." It was assumed that an inmate would only talk to a guard to rat someone out. However, I couldn't help but think that the guards did notice that I had no food in my pan, but no one said or did anything.

One of the first and most obvious things I noticed after being marched off to cell house six was that no one spoke to me other than to mutter a threat as they passed near me. Some of the inmates might have had something to say to me, but being seen talking to me would jeopardize their standing in the population, and no inmate could afford that.

When it was time for evening lock up ("Rack 'em") a loud buzzer sounded. Each inmate had about a minute to get into his cell. The cell doors were mechanically operated by the guard pulling a large lever from the inside of the guard cage at the end of the tier. The noise was deafening. The heavy chain attached at the top of each door would clang through the heavy steel channel to close the cell doors. The doors were all slammed closed with a tremendous thud. The loud bang of the closed doors was followed by a brief period of complete and utter silence. I felt an eerie chill of being abandoned. It seemed so final, so permanent.

As frightening as the locking of the doors sounded, ironically, it brought some degree of security to me. My door was locked, I was no longer vulnerable to the other inmates. I could let my guard down and relax a little from the constant worry and fear that someone would shank me in the back with a piece of cold metal that had been honed sharp by rubbing it on the concrete floor.

That night my sleep came only in very small pieces. The cell house was very noisy. The loud banging of the heavy iron doors clanged open and shut even during the night making sleep impossible. Individual cell doors could be opened as needed. Some inmates worked at jobs with around the clock hours such as the hospital, the officers' mess (kitchen help) and the coal plant. Doors were opened for these men when they went to work or when they returned.

When inmates walked down my tier they shuffled their feet as they passed my cell. Many threw notes in my cell with threats of a terrible death. I was alone; I felt vulnerable. I was terrified. I thought that prisoners were supposed to be sent to prison as punishment, not for punishment.

Most of the night I laid awake and thought to myself, "I'm in too deep this time. I'll never get out." I did not believe I would survive. I felt abandoned and forsaken. I was tired and hungry. When I did sleep, I had horrific nightmares. Sleep awoke the demons that I wanted so desperately to forget. I would wake up in a panic. The nightmares were exhausting; they were more real than life.

Friday morning when the chow bell rang for breakfast a cold chill came over me. I marched off to the chow hall only to be left with an empty pan once again. Lunch and supper were no different. I did manage to grab some bread near the end of the line from the unattended bread table at lunch time. I had hoped I could do the same thing at the evening meal, but it did not work.

On Friday evening, just before lights out, an inmate stopped in front of my cell. The inmate wore prison number 31595 on his shirt. I looked up at the man in total disbelief. My blood ran cold. I recognized him immediately. It was Don Zorens. He was the man I had hunted and wanted to kill when I was a rookie recruit. My attitude toward this man suddenly changed. I had become the hunted. I felt real fear.

"How's it going?" he asked.

I could not speak.

"Don't let these guys fuck you over, Winstanley," he said.

"Here, I brought you something," he said, as he reached in between the bars. He handed me a sandwich wrapped in a piece of brown paper towel. I reached out and took it. "Hang in there," he said, and walked away. I looked at the sandwich. It was meatloaf. My eyes welled up with tears. My hands shook from fear and hunger. I broke the sandwich up in three or four pieces and flushed it down my toilet. I was so paranoid, I knew someone was trying to poison me.

PUTA

Saturday morning brought new fear. Again I had no breakfast. Most of the inmates did not have jobs to go to on Saturday. They continued to shuffle by my cell. Sometimes I felt they were just going back and forth. They had a variety of comments to make as they passed. Many of the Mexicans called me "puta." Being called "puta" did not bother me in the least. I didn't know what it meant. I told myself that was a very nice thing and that they must love me. Much later, I discovered that "puta" is the Spanish word for whore.

At lunch, I got no food, but I managed to get some bread again. The bread table at the end of the line was not always manned. Sometime after lunch it was time to go to the yard. The warden had warned me about going to the yard, but I decided to go anyway. If they were going to kill me then let's get it on. I could no longer stay in my cell; I had to get out. When the bell rang for yard, I walked out of my cell as tall as I could and went with all the other inmates to the yard.

The yard was a large outdoor open area much like a huge playground or a big ball field. There were a lot of activities.

There were some bleachers along one side where inmates played cards or dominoes or just sat and talked. There was an area for weight lifting with barbells and benches. Others played catch with a baseball. There was a volleyball game at one end. The sun was shining and it was a warm day. There were more inmates than usual in the yard that afternoon. There was a large oval in the yard paved with cinders for track events. Some of the inmates walked the track. I joined in walking the track. The other walkers distanced themselves a bit from me, not wanting to give the appearance of being with me. My going to the yard took everyone by complete surprise. The other inmates were in disbelief. No one would ever suspect that I would do anything that foolish. I must have walked that oval a hundred times. Other inmates watched me, but no one came close. I'm sure that the guards in the towers surrounding the yard were watching my every step. When the bell sounded that yard was over, I walked back to the cell house as if I had been doing it forever.

That night, as I lay on my bunk with my eyes closed, I pictured all the food on the steam table in the chow hall. It seemed the inmates ate pretty well—all except me, of course. There seemed to be a variety of wholesome food. There was meat and vegetables and grain and all the good things that made for a well balanced and nutritious diet. I thought to myself that most of the inmates probably did not eat that well three times a day ever before in their miserable lives, unless of course they were in jail someplace.

My mother, whom I loved dearly, was a devout Catholic. She would mail me a religious card two or three times each week with a picture of The Blessed Virgin Mary or Jesus on the front and an appropriate message on the inside. At the bottom of each card she would always write, "Try not to think." Love, Mother. It made me laugh inside. How do you go about trying not to think? I always wanted to write back and say, "Not thinking is what got me in here in the first place."

STEAK

The breakfast on Sunday morning did not look all that appetizing. Perhaps I had gone so long without real food that the breakfast just didn't look like something I wanted to eat. It really didn't make any difference, I didn't get any.

At lunch on Sunday it was a different matter. I was hungry and desperate. I followed the line of men down the endless aisle looking straight ahead trying to keep the tears that were welling up inside from falling. I must hold my head up high. I must not let them see me cry, please, God, not one tear drop. I felt sorry for myself. I was so discouraged, and I had never been this hungry. As the line moved along the steam table I saw a big pan of meat. Sunday dinner was always special. Today it was chicken fried steak. I stopped the line. I refused to move. I stared at the inmate with the tongs who was supposed to put a piece of meat on my pan. The line started to back up. There were a couple of screws (Screw is prison slang for guard) with Winchester model 97 twelve gauge shotguns on the catwalk overhead in the chow hall. These guards started toward the steam table to see what the commotion was. The inmate with the tongs in his hand realized there was going to be trouble and he put a steak on my pan. Wow, I could hardly believe that it worked. I stopped the line. I had a steak. At the center of the steam table, where the line split for going to our seat, another inmate spit on my steak.

I was so mad I was shaking. I didn't even see the inmate that spit. I just heard him spit and saw it land on my steak. I made my way to my seat on the bench. I cut the part of the steak with the spit on it away with my spoon, and ate the rest. I thought that no person should have to be treated like this. This was unimaginable hell.

Sunday supper was cold cuts. Sunday supper was always cold cuts. I smiled when I went through the chow line and stopped at every place along the line that had something I wanted. It worked pretty well. By the end of the line, I had quite a full pan, and some butterscotch pudding for dessert!

The chow hall situation got better. The inmates who worked in the kitchen knew they had a sought after job. They did not want to get in trouble and run the risk of losing their assignment. There were still some inmates that passed me by when they were handing out the food, but for the most part the inmates reluctantly put something on my pan. If there was something I really wanted, I would stop the line and refuse to go on. That usually did the trick and I got served.

At the evening meal one Sunday the dessert being offered was cherry pie. Someone remembering the headlines in the morning papers of January that year reminded the other inmates about my confessing for a slice of cherry pie. The inmate who was dishing it out from the big pie pan and the other inmates around him were all whispering as I got near.

They were warning everyone not to eat the cherry pie because it contained sodium pentothal.

IT'S OFF TO WORK WE GO

On Monday morning, I started a new "career." My job assignment was the hill gang. All new inmates entering the population worked on the hill gang for thirty days. There were 25 or 30 inmates in this group. Each morning after breakfast we reported to the west gate where we lined up in double file to be counted and to have our number recorded. When the guards were satisfied that everyone who was supposed be there was there, the gate was opened, and we marched out under the watchful eyes of the well-armed guards in the tower above.

We walked about a half mile up the hill behind the prison to a pile of shovels and picks and wheelbarrows. We chipped away at the mountain with picks and then used the shovel to put the rocks in the wheelbarrow. We then wheeled the rocks about 100 yards to dump them into another pile. It was hard physical work, but it was just busy work. Inmates had been chipping away at that mountain for decades and had only scratched the surface.

At about noon, some inmates accompanied by a guard pulled a wagon up to us with sack lunches and big containers of Kool Aid. There were a lot of complaints about the sandwiches made with lunch meat, but I thought it was wonderful.

While working on the hill gang, I witnessed a rather bizarre incident. There was a fellow named John who was the most obnoxious, disgusting individual I had ever met. He was the king of four letter words. I never heard such a foul mouth. I thought perhaps he wanted to come across as some kind of bad ass as a defense mechanism by pretending to be some kind of tough guy with all his filthy language. Working with us on the hill gang was a rather quiet somewhat small Hispanic fellow named Carlos. John took every opportunity to bad mouth Carlos. He constantly ragged on him about his mother and sister and all of his ancestors. Carlos finally reached his limit one afternoon and swung a pick ax hitting John on the side of the head just behind the left eye. John's eye was pushed out and was protruding from its socket with blood squirting everywhere.

As John reached up with his hand and felt his eye protruding from his face, he dropped to his knees and began to summon help from God. I was dumbfounded. From the same mouth where all the filth came, I heard the most eloquent plea to Heaven I had ever heard. John's prayer sounded something like: "Dear merciful God in heaven, I beseech thee in Christ's name for help in my time of need. In the name of the Holy Father, forgive me my sins. Please help me, dear Lord. I'll never do another bad thing if you will only help me this one time. Dear God, don't let me lose my eye. Please, oh please, dear God, help me."

Why in moments of crisis do we ask God for strength and help? Many people don't pray or talk to God on a regular basis. It's only when things go wrong and we're left with no place to turn that we turn to God. Author and philosopher Voltaire said: "If God did not exist it would be necessary to invent him."

A man once told me he thought Jesus must hang out at prisons because a lot of people find him there.

Why would we ask something that may well be a figment of our imaginations for guidance? Why are we not strong enough to search inside ourselves for the power to overcome?

Later I heard that John had been transferred to the prison unit at the State Hospital in Pueblo. I don't know if Carlos was prosecuted.

The humiliating aspect of my new career of working on the hill gang was that at about three thirty when our day was over, we had to pass through the west gate again to get back into the main prison. This meant stripping completely naked in a small room and having to stand there with our arms extended while the guards looked everywhere they could think to look. The most degrading part of all of this is when the guard would holler, "Bend over and spread 'em." The inmates were dirty and sweaty; the stench alone was pretty hard to take. We then walked through some type of portal that supposedly detected any contraband. After all of our clothes were searched, we were told to get dressed and line up along the wall. After all the inmates were dressed we were checked off from a list the guard had and told to return to our respective cell houses.

I did find one benefit to this job. It was physically hard and tiring work. I was able to sleep even with all the cell house noise and the banging of the doors.

As you can imagine, the inmates created a number of problems for me because I had been a policeman. I took it personally because their acts of hatred were directed at me, when in fact it was what I had been or what I had represented that caused them to react the way they did.

One problem that was particularly annoying was the laundry. Each inmate went to the laundry twice a week. I don't know how it was determined which days or time an inmate was assigned to go, but the group I was assigned to went at 4:10 p.m. on Tuesday and Friday. I dreaded laundry day. It was not only where they did laundry, it was also where we showered. The old timers used to say if you drop the soap in the shower, you better kick it all the way to Pueblo before you pick it up. They said this precaution was necessary to avoid being harpooned by a "rump ranger." Just outside the shower room we put all our clothes, including what we were wearing, into a large laundry basket and went to the showers.

After showering we walked through a tray of blue liquid that was supposed to kill any type of foot fungus or athlete's foot. We then picked up a towel and went to the counter where an inmate laundry worker gave us two changes of clothes including socks and underwear. There were bins behind the counter with inmate's numbers on them. The bin marked 33123 was always empty. I think it is safe to say that the inmates who worked in the laundry had my number. My clothes always disappeared. This meant that I would have to stand there naked for 30 minutes or sometimes an hour and wait for the laundry crew to find some other clothes and stencil my number on them. The clothes they gave me never fit. They were either far too big or so small that I could not get them buttoned.

SOCIAL STRATUM

Our society has a tendency to judge people by their position or wealth rather than the quality of their character.

The pecking order in a prison is far more defining. It is based on how bad you are or how bad the crime was that put you there. Murderers are usually the alpha dogs in prison, whereas the bottom of the social ladder is reserved for rapists and child molesters. However, there is a special place on the very bottom reserved for an ex-policeman, especially one who has been labeled as a stool pigeon.

After my thirty days on the hill gang, I was given a new assignment. I got a pretty good job compared to some. Because I had graduated high school and could type, I was assigned to the fingerprints and records division in the main administration building.

New inmates were fingerprinted on a dozen official fingerprint cards. All the information on the inmate was then typed on each card from the master card. These cards were distributed to state and local law enforcement agencies as well as the FBI and other federal government bureaus. Most of my job had to do with typing these cards.

There was some improvement with the difficulties I had being in prison after I got the job in the administration building. The laundry situation improved because the inmates who worked in the main administration building got starch in their shirts and got their clothes pressed. This was done by a different section of the laundry facility, and I did not have so much trouble. I had learned by now that a couple of packs of cigarettes to the right guy helped things run a whole lot smoother.

I also discovered that I had a most unexpected ally—a true friend who took it upon himself to help me and keep me safe. It was Don Zorens. Don was the big man in cell house six. He was looked up to because he had murdered a cop. He was captain of the prison football team. He worked in the officers' mess. He was the man. Not much went down in cell house six that Don did not know about.

He was the man who, just a few years earlier, I wanted so desperately to kill so that I might look like a hero. I never knew why he decided to befriend me, but as sure as I sit here today, he saved my life again and again. Perhaps he felt remorse for killing a Denver policeman with a wife and six children. Maybe he thought it would look good on his record. For whatever reason, I am eternally grateful.

Two inmates threw benzene in my cell followed by some burning newspaper. Benzene is a clear flammable liquid that inmates used in a tool for wood burning and as fuel in cigarette lighters. Don Zorens was the only person to holler loud enough for the guard to get my door open so I did not suffocate to death. Other inmates in the prison were making bets and laying odds betting cigarettes that I wouldn't make it six months.

I was attacked while I was in the barber chair in cell house six. An inmate who went by the name "Teabags" had concealed a home-made shank under his coat. He approached me from behind. The knife was made from a six inch piece of steel pipe. Don Zorens was nearby, and realizing what was about to happen, pushed the inmate away; the shank fell to the floor.

I talked with Don Zorens the day after he intervened in the attempt to kill me.

"Hey, Don, I think you saved my ass yesterday," I said.

"It's cool man, we don't need the hassle in six," he said.

(Meaning that there would be unnecessary heat brought to cell house six with a stabbing.)

Don took it upon himself to walk near me when it was time to go to the chow hall. Because of the respect Don had among the other inmates, the others backed off some, and my life got a whole lot easier. I suspect that the sandwich Don had offered me a few months earlier was an act of kindness and was not poisoned as I had feared.

I don't think I ever talked to Don Zorens again. He was eventually released from prison and married a nun whom he met while in a prison. She did prison ministry work. She left the church and they were married shortly after his release. They had two children together. Zorens died of heart disease in 1989 according to the Denver Post.

I never told Don Zorens of my desire to kill him a few years earlier. It didn't seem appropriate, or perhaps I just lacked the courage. I certainly did not want to do anything that might jeopardize the help he was giving me or destroy our relationship.

LET'S FIGHT

The institution had a policy whereby if an inmate had a disagreement with another inmate, he could go to the midway after breakfast and "call out" the other person. The midway was a small building near the center of the prison grounds where each inmate was to stop and show his pass before proceeding to his next destination. The midway was the clearing house for the prison to keep track of who was going where. An inmate could not pass from one part of the prison to another without stopping at midway and showing his pass.

Calling another inmate out meant that the two inmates were escorted by a guard to the gym where the inmates put on a pair of lightweight boxing gloves and got into the ring to fight. There were no rounds or time limits. The two prisoners just slugged it out until one inmate could no longer fight. The one left standing was presumed the winner. The idea of this policy was to have a way for inmates to settle their differences before problems could escalate to much bigger problems such as stabbings or even riots. If an inmate was "called out" and refused to go fight, he was an automatic loser.

I discovered that this was my salvation. Whenever an inmate would say something derogatory to me or push me, I would try to get his number so I could call him out. I was careful never to choose an inmate who was smaller than I was. I didn't want the inmates to say I was picking on the little guys. There was no shortage of candidates; I always had a list. I was not what the inmates referred to as a "cherry." I had fought in the Golden Gloves program when I was young, and of course I did my share of fighting as a policeman. I did pretty well, but I did not always win. I got my ass whipped real good a few times. However, I discovered that it was not whether you won or lost, but that you were willing to fight that made the difference. Even when I lost, I fought as hard as I could, and that seemed to earn a certain degree of respect.

If an inmate went to the ring with me and lost, it was difficult for him to hold his head up. The dirty remarks cast toward me nearly stopped because the inmates realized that there was a possibility that I would get their number and call them out. If an inmate went to the ring with me and I got in a few lucky punches and the inmate lost to that "rat cop" he could be ostracized and humiliated by his peers in the population. Not many of them wanted to risk that. Convicts are a bit like a pack of wild dogs. As a group they can be a threat, but for the most part, alone and singled out, they're cowards.

Life got a lot easier for me when I started calling someone out nearly every morning. Occasionally, I would get beat up to the point that my eyes were swollen shut, but I would still manage to get to my job and sit at my typewriter at the fingerprint bureau. If I did not report to my assignment, it was viewed as an admission to a total loss or surrender, which I was not willing to do. On the few mornings when I could not see well enough to type, the manager of the fingerprint division, Mr. Manley, would divide up the cards I was supposed to do among the other inmates in the typing pool in the office. They would not be happy about doing the extra work, but they would not complain to me for fear of their being called out when I got better.

My willingness to fight was the key to my survival and peace of mind. It did more than anything else to help me cope and gain some respect among the other prisoners.

MORE ARRESTS

Although I was the first Denver police officer arrested and sent to prison, the investigation was ongoing. A few other police officers had been arrested, but it was only the tip of the iceberg.

As an inmate in the state penitentiary, I did not have access to television, but I did manage to get the Denver daily newspapers on a fairly regular basis. It was interesting to read the stories as they unfolded each day in the papers. There was so much going on that it became difficult to keep track of the cast of characters. A few more policemen were arrested each week or two. Some of the police officers who were arrested were from other district stations and I had no knowledge that they were involved in any burglaries.

Shortly after the investigation began, District Attorney Bert Keating had convened a special grand jury. The grand jury heard from sixty-nine witnesses over a period of nearly four months. No Denver police officers were indicted. The "code of silence" seemed to prevail. District Attorney Keating said,

"Witnesses lost their memories, evaded questions and refused to cooperate."

The citizens of Denver were outraged at the police and the administration. The Rocky Mountain News claimed "Whitewash." The Denver Post reported that the corruption went much deeper, and that not enough was being done to get to the bottom of the problem. Governor McNichols and Mayor Batterton asked for an outside special prosecutor to head up the investigation.

In June of 1961, after I had been in prison for nearly four months, Richard Kuykendall, who was the chief of police in Commerce City, got a reliable tip that burglars were going to break into the King Soopers store in Commerce City on Thursday, June 19. Commerce City is located in Adams County and joins Denver on the north. Chief Kuykendall called Division Chief Walter Nelson who was in charge of the Denver police burglary investigation for help because the Commerce City police department consisted of only seven officers. On the night in question, five Denver detectives led by Captain Jack Haeflinger responded and took up positions nearby. Kuykendall and his officers hid in the basement. Three men arrived and quickly broke through the ceiling and dropped into the store. The trap was sprung as the burglars attempted to open the safe. The three men arrested turned out to be present or former Denver policemen. A fourth suspect, acting as a lookout parked in the getaway vehicle nearby, sped away when the plan went sour and he managed to escape capture.

The focus of the investigation in Adams County seemed to center around who the tipster was and how he knew, and who the driver of the getaway car was, rather than the aborted King Soopers' safe job itself.

During this time, a fierce political battle was brewing in Adams County. The sheriff was soon to be up for re-election. It was alleged that someone trying to dig up some dirt on Adams County Sheriff Robert Roberts was snooping around his house late one evening, and actually overheard the sheriff in the dining room of his home. He and some others were planning the burglary.

Because the Denver police burglary investigation had now crossed county lines, the state entered the investigation. A few days later Colorado Attorney General Duke Dunbar suggested that a high-ranking law officer may have been the missing King Soopers getaway driver. A car had been observed in the King Soopers vicinity a few minutes before the break-in, and the same car was spotted near the scene of another safecracking a week earlier. The license plates were traced to a police undercover car used by the Adams County Sheriff's Department. Three weeks later, July 25, 1961, Adams County Sheriff Bob Roberts, an ex FBI agent, was arrested and charged in connection with the foiled King Soopers burglary. Bob Roberts was later convicted and sent to the State Penitentiary.

BLACK SATURDAY

By September 1961, a total of thirteen police officers had been arrested and indicted on a variety of charges relating to burglary and safecracking. One of the officers, Gerald "Jerry" Sanford, who was reported to be one of the more prolific and brazen police burglars, had been convicted on several counts, and was to be sentenced by Denver District Judge George McNamara.

Judge McNamara, a former police officer himself, was able to do what the grand jury and all of the special investigators could not get done. On September 15, 1961, Gerald Sanford appeared before Judge McNamara for sentencing on the burglary and safe job of the U.S. Loan Company. The honorable judge surprised everyone in the community when he sentenced Sanford to 10 to 32 years of hard labor in the state penitentiary. The unusually stiff sentence given Sanford sent an enormous shock wave to the other policemen who had been arrested or were awaiting trial or sentencing.

Sanford, who had until now refused to discuss anything with the special investigators or district attorney, abruptly changed his tune about "talking" and begged for mercy.

One of the state investigators was quoted as saying, "After McNamara racked Sanford, it was standing room only in the confessional." As Fran Lebowitz said in her book <u>Social Studies</u>, "Spilling your guts is just exactly as charming as it sounds."

The effect of this was like a snowball rolling downhill. By the end of the month this avalanche resulted in criminal cases being prepared against an additional twenty-two police burglars, bringing the total to thirty-five.

September 30, 1961, will long be remembered as "Black Saturday" in the annals of Denver history. It was a particularly dark day for the men and women of the Denver Police Department. In a room in the state capital, each of the accused was brought in turn before Chief of Police James Childers and other members of the department. Each was requested to turn in his badge and police equipment. They were then marched single file to waiting vans for transport to the city jail while the citizens of Denver watched. The Denver newspapers were full of pictures of the officers being charged. It was said that the serious degree of corruption permeating the Denver Police Department had finally been realized.

A week after "Black Saturday," Chief James Childers retired from the department. I was saddened to see him go in shame and disgrace the way he did. He had served the city of Denver with an unblemished record for forty years. He was a fine gentleman and well liked by the department and the community. I found it hard to imagine the fact that he had been a Denver policeman long before I was born. Chief Childers evidently had no knowledge of the police burglary rings operating during his command. On the other hand, it was later determined that the Denver Police Department had been sweeping its dirt under the rug for decades.

The Denver Police Department became the brunt of cruel jokes and ridicule. It was a difficult time for the honest hard working men and women of the law enforcement community.

That year the annual "Frontier Days" rodeo in Cheyenne, Wyoming, hosted a delegation from Denver sponsored by the Denver Post. Over 500 of Denver's prominent citizens had been transported to Cheyenne as a group on a special train. Internationally, it was the time of the Cuban missile crisis. In opening the festivities of the day in Cheyenne, the rodeo announcer joked, "I understand President Kennedy is considering two alternatives as a way out of the current troubles with Castro. One is to ask his dad to buy Cuba; the other is to get the Denver police to steal it."

CELL HOUSE SIX

After "Black Saturday" my fellow inmates in cell house six gave me flack about all the "dirty" cops. I would hear them shout things like, "Hey, Winstanley, you had better make room for your buddies, they're all coming down here to see you." And, "Won't it be nice to have a bunch of rat bastard cops down here with us."

After I had lived in cell house six for a couple of months things seemed to get a little better for me. The other inmates didn't hassle me as much. I think my rather aggressive attitude toward the other inmates in not allowing them to bully me or intimidate me was the key to helping me to be able to do my time a little easier.

Cell house six was the oldest cell house still being used at the prison. The cells were very small and were only one man cells that measured about eight and a half by six feet. I was able to get somewhat friendly with my neighbors, and sometimes at night I would talk to the men who occupied the cells on either side of mine.

Big Denny lived in the cell on one side of me. He was 19 years old, and had been in prison only a year or two. He had been convicted of manslaughter after beating another young man to death in a fit of rage after a football game. He had been sentenced to 25 years. I felt sorry for Big Denny because he never got mail, and no one ever came to visit him. He never talked about having a family. He seemed like a nice young man.

Big Denny worked in the tailor shop, and was paid ten cents a day. His fifty cents a week went for personal care items, and left no room for his tobacco habit. The institution gave him tobacco each week, but it was just dried leaf tobacco. He had to crumble it up and roll his own cigarettes. The canteen sold Zig-Zag and Tip-Top papers for rolling your own cigarettes. The papers cost a nickel. Evidently, that was more than Big Denny thought he could afford. During a routine search of his cell, the guards discovered that he had gotten a bible from the chaplin's office, and was cutting little strips of it to roll cigarettes. This had been going on for some time because by the time the guards discovered what he was doing, he had smoked up Luke, John and most of Jeremiah. The other inmates in the cell house started calling their cigarettes little Deuteronomies. Big Denny had the only cigarettes that had writing from one end to the other.

The fellow who occupied the cell on the other side of mine was Charlie Gray Fox, or "Sir Charles" as he preferred to be called. I don't know where he got a name like Gray Fox. I don't think he was an American Indian. Sir Charles was thought of as a total wacko by the other inmates because he usually had an imaginary dog he called Duke on an imaginary leash that he led around the prison wherever he went. I didn't think Sir Charles was crazy at all. I think it was a defense mechanism. The other inmates pretty much left Charlie alone because he was thought of as a nut case. That's just the way Charlie wanted it. When other people talked about him, they referred to him as "that crazy bastard with the dog." I spent a lot of time talking with Sir Charles; he was no dummy.

After "lights out" many evenings I could hear Charlie very softly singing to his imaginary waitress about food that we did not see in jail. I would stand as close as I could in the front corner of my cell to listen to his words. It has been a long time, and I can't remember it all, but one song went:

> I'd like some tuna salad,
> On a piece of sour dough,
> With a little bit of lettuce,
> And a dab of mayo.

> I'll have a bag of chips,
> And another cup of joe,
> I'll just eat it here thanks,
> I've got no place to go.

Charlie wrote poetry. Many times he would pass one of his poems over for me to read. They were wonderful. I have lost many of them along the way, but there is one that I have kept.

YOUR LITTLE EVIL WISHES
by: Sir Charles Gray Fox

When your little evil wishes,
Have all come home to roost,
And the law of Colorado,
Has finally turned me loose.

In your Cadillac you're wooing,
Your million-dollar friends,
While I'm working for a dime a day,
In the Canon City Pen

The letters that you write me,
Once a year or so,
Read, darling, I'm so sorry,
But I just ran out of dough.

When this bum rap is over,
In fifteen years or more,
In a cheap suit I'll come courtin',
Round about your door.

You went to see my lawyer;
You say he wasn't in;
The boys sure keep you busy,
In your night life drinking wine.

You've forgotten me, my darling,
Though my money you still spend,
And your little evil wishes,
Have sent me to the Pen.

BEING LOCKED UP

Being sent to prison has many different effects on people. The loss of freedom and being separated from friends and family creates the most difficulties. Many inmates miss their access to liquor or to drugs. Others are more bothered by the lack of intimacy or sex.

Often when people meet someone who has been in prison they wonder about sex. Most people are not so direct as to come right out and ask, but they wonder about what you did or how you handled it. We hear stories about sex in prison from watching movies or television that would lead us to believe that if you go to prison you are destined to be raped. In general, society has the perception that sodomy is a common practice among prison inmates. Of course this does happen, but I don't believe it is as widespread as the prison dramas we see might indicate.

Homosexual activity is more prevalent among long term inmates and lifers than it is among inmates during shorter sentences. It is obvious that the longer a person is locked up the more thought he might give to some alternatives to masturbation. The intimacy or closeness of another person seems to be as important as the act of sex itself. Some inmates are what I refer to as "situational sexual." They are not gay, they just take whatever is handy. Some inmates claim to have been forced into a sexual relationship or sexual activity to cover up the fact that they were willing participants.

There are instances of a young small "pretty" inmate becoming the sexual property of a much stronger prison leader. The frail or young inmate in this situation usually does not like the arrangement but needs to comply for his own protection and to avoid being abused by the general population. The stronger more seasoned inmate takes care of and protects his "bitch."

I knew of two inmates (both doing long sentences) that became so enamored with each other that they had matching rings made by an inmate metal worker and exchanged vows in the chapel in the presence of some of their inmate friends. They made no secret of their affection for one another, although being open about a love affair with another inmate was not well accepted in the sixties.

This kind of behavior is against prison policy, but the prison guards and staff know that it is going on, and there is little they can do to stop it.

As for me, it was not an issue because nobody wanted anything to do with me sexually or otherwise.

Of course I missed my freedom and family, but I was haunted by the shame I had brought on myself and the people who loved me. One of the things that bothered me was not being able to fix things around the house. My wife would write or tell me about something at home that was broken or about something that wasn't working on the car. I felt frustrated and helpless. I've always taken pride in being mechanical and able to fix things around the house. I had the tools and the ability and knew exactly what the problem was and how to fix it, but I couldn't. I wanted to tell the guard to just let me run home and make the needed repairs and that I would come right back...And I would have...Well, maybe not right straight back.

One of the most difficult things about going to prison is being removed from society. That's what prisons do. Criminals are placed in prisons to protect society. We are all, however, social animals. We need to communicate. We need to share our thoughts, our emotions, and our experiences. We need to feel needed and a part of something. It is what makes us human. That is why we live in communities and towns. We join groups and organizations. We form fraternal brotherhoods and fellowship groups. We go to church and join clubs.

If someone goes off to be by himself and isolates himself from others with little or no contact, he is considered to be an outcast or to be weird. At the end of the day we need to confide in someone. We need someone who will listen to us because they care.

When a person is removed from his friends and family by being sent to prison it leaves an enormous social and emotional void. The prison systems do not address these issues. There is little support. Some prisoners have no family and no one comes to visit. They receive no mail and appear to have no contact with anyone on the outside. They seem lost. Loneliness is the ultimate poverty.

Many prisons offer drug rehab or Alcoholics Anonymous programs, but these programs often fall short of the social needs of many prisoners. As a result, inmates who are incarcerated for long periods of time join prison gangs. Others may turn to some type of deviant sexual behavior. Many turn to religion or worship in some type of cult. They all want to belong to something in an attempt to feel needed or validate their existence.

Inmates were allowed two visits per week. My wife made the two hour drive down to the prison when she could, usually about twice a month. The visiting room left much to be desired. It was humiliating for people who came to visit because they were thoroughly searched by the guards. We sat on small stools and visited through a heavy closed meshed screen. It was noisy and crowded. Although I missed seeing my children, I asked her not to bring the kids because I felt too ashamed and did not want them to see me in jail.

Inmate phone calls were not permitted except in an emergency, such as a death in the family. An inmate had to get permission to make a call, and to have sufficient funds in his inmate account to cover the cost of the call. All telephone calls were monitored by a guard on an extension phone.

There are some inmates that seem to do quite well in prison. They still bitch and complain because that's what is expected. The truth is that many of them never had three well balanced meals every day or a warm bed every night in their life. Many inmates seem to thrive in a structured atmosphere where a regimented routine must be followed. Obviously, some people are not good at making choices. Making bad choices is usually what brought them to prison in the first place. Prison life does not allow for a lot of choices and some people seem to do better in prison than out.

If the guards were to all go on strike and leave the gate open, many of the inmates would not leave. Sadly, they don't have any place to go. They would have to make choices. Where would they eat? Where would they sleep? Who would take care of them? I suspect that many who would run out when the gate was open would soon return.

CLASSIFICATION BOARD

I had served less than seven months of my sentence when I was notified that I was going to meet the classification board. This came as a very unexpected and pleasant surprise. Normally an inmate does not meet the classification board until he has served at least a year or a good part of his sentence. Each inmate who meets the board is given a classification in accordance to his risk factor. The board takes into consideration how an inmate has adjusted to prison, his attitude, how much time he has left to serve and his record of any violent behavior or sex-related offenses.

If an inmate has a clean record during his time in prison and has no history of behavior involving violence or sexual offenses, he is considered for trustee status by the classification board. There were three categories: high, medium and minimum. High-risk inmates were not allowed outside the main prison. The medium-risk category could be sent to the new medium security prison outside the main walls. About half of the prison population was doing their time outside the main prison walls. Minimum security meant that you were eligible to go to one of the many outside facilities. This included the garden, dairy, ranch, slaughter house, honor farm, warden's residence (maintenance) and a few other places.

I was summoned to the classification board at an early date because I was a nuisance. I had followed all the rules, but my presence in the institution was disruptive. None of the other inmates wanted to be near me or even work in my area. The guards had to watch me more closely than the other inmates because there had been two attempts on my life There was no doubt that my presence in the prison was the cause of a great deal of tension.

The day after I met the classification board I was notified that I would be transferred to the ranch on Friday. Early on Friday morning I had all my stuff packed in one cardboard box and was ready to go. After breakfast, I got my box and was checked out of cell house six and reported to the west gate to await the big green prison bus for transportation to the ranch.

The ride on the bus was very pleasant. Part of the ride went through the town of Canon City. Being able to see people along the road, and cars going by was delightful. I felt a certain amount of freedom just being able to ride along and look out the window without being shackled or in handcuffs. The ride seemed to take a long time because after the bus drove onto prison property, it made several stops. First it was the garden. The next stop was the dairy. The bus delivered the mail and other prison paperwork as well as shuttling inmates to and from the main prison. Prisoners rode the bus to take care of a variety of other business such as parole hearings or medical visits. I estimated the ranch to be about ten miles from the main prison.

THE RANCH

The bus finally pulled up to a one story white stucco building with a lawn and trees and bushes just like you might imagine around a country ranch house. The guard driving the bus announced it was the Ranch. I picked up my box of belongings and made my way to the front of the bus and got off. Of course the prison grapevine had made everyone aware of my being sent to the Ranch long before I arrived.

I made my way up the walk to the porch in front of the building. As I started up the three or four steps I noticed a rather fat Mexican man sitting on the porch rail. I later learned his name was Zapata. As I walked up, the man said, "I thought someone would have killed your sorry ass before now." A lot of thoughts went through my mind. What should I do? If I got into trouble before I got in the door, I might lose my chance to get outside the walls. On the other hand, I had promised myself that I was not going to "bitch up" or be intimidated. Without a word, I sat my box down and turned toward the man and hit him as hard as I could square in the face. The force of my blow knocked him over the rail and into the bushes below. I picked up my box and went inside to the office for check in. Although everyone knew what had happened, I never heard a word about the incident. During the next year and a half that I lived at the ranch, Zapata and I never spoke, and no one ever said anything bad about me, at least not to my face.

Compared to "Old Max," the main prison, the Ranch was a slice of heaven. The tension that is present inside the main walls brought on by the hostility and bitterness of hard core criminals makes it a frightening and difficult place for everyone. There is a different class of inmate outside the main walls. Inmates who have any acts of violence or escape on their record are not eligible for assignment outside the main prison. The minimum security inmates who are transferred to one of the outside facilities were usually "short-timers." Short-timer meant the inmate usually had less than five years of his sentence left to serve. They have hope.

There were approximately 90 inmates assigned to the Ranch. The population varied from time to time as inmates were released, and others came.

Much was being done to try to make the prison system more cost effective. There was constant pressure from the Colorado legislature to cut costs and make the prison system more cost effective and self supporting. In many areas the prison was somewhat effective at this. The prison operated a large slaughter house. This combined with the Garden, the Ranch and the Dairy, all operated by prisoners, supplied nearly all the food for the main prison and the State Hospital at Pueblo,

Colorado. Food was also supplied for the State Reformatory at Buena Vista. Inside the main prison, there was a cannery, a tailor shop and a furniture factory. State license plates and road signs were produced in the tag plant. All of the work was done with inmate labor.

The Ranch was bordered by the Arkansas River on the east, and covered about 40 square miles. That's approximately 25,000 acres.

THE PONY MOTOR

A day or two after I arrived, the number one "cat skinner" at the ranch was paroled. I felt as though I had really lucked out in that I was assigned to the tractor barn and was told that I would be working on a D-6 Caterpillar tractor. A good bulldozer man is called a "cat skinner." As far back as I could remember, as with many young boys, I was fascinated by big tractors and heavy equipment. Now I was going to learn to be a "cat skinner." I thought that perhaps being sentenced to hard labor would not be so bad after all.

All of the inmates who worked on the big John Deere tractors and heavy equipment bunked in the tractor barn which was just across the road from the main ranch building. There were 12 or 14 of us in there. It was rather primitive. There was a big wood- burning stove in the middle of the room for heat. We had to go across the road to the main dormitory building at the Ranch to use the toilet and get our meals. The other men in the tractor barn seemed rather cordial toward me. I did not feel unwelcome; at least they talked to me and were not openly hostile.

On Monday morning after breakfast, I rode on the fuel buggy to the field to start my job on one of the two D-6 Caterpillars at the prison Ranch. An old inmate who was called "Curley" was assigned to teach me what I needed to know. Curley knew a lot about Caterpillar tractors. Curley was missing his left hand just above the wrist. He lost the hand at Guadalcanal in the Pacific during the Second World War. When it was cold, he put a big wool sock over the stump for warmth. Over the next few months he taught me many valuable lessons; I learned them well. Curley made me laugh. He always seemed happy and had a broad smile. He was one of those people you meet in life that you never forget. Curley used to tell me that everything in life is more enjoyable if you're not overly invested in the outcome. When I first met Curley, I couldn't imagine how he could operate a bull dozer with only one hand. As it turned out, he was better at it with one hand than I was with two.

In order to get the tractor started, first the pony motor had to be started. The pony motor was the starter motor attached to the main diesel engine of the Caterpillar. The pony motor was similar to a large gasoline lawn mower engine. It had to be started by wrapping the starter pulley with a rope and then pulling the rope hard to spin the engine fast enough to get it started. Just getting the pony motor started on some cold winter mornings was a difficult job. After the pony motor was running well, there was a lever that engaged it with a fly wheel. Then another lever was used to slowly clutch the spinning fly wheel and engage it with the main diesel engine to get it turning enough to start the diesel engine on the Cat.

When the Caterpillar was not being used as a bulldozer, it was used to pull a scraper, sometimes referred to as a bucker or a can. The scraper was a large piece of machinery with huge rubber tires that held six cubic yards of dirt. The scraper was lowered to the ground and drug behind the Caterpillar to get filled with dirt. When it was time to empty the dirt out, a large section of the scraper was activated to push the dirt out like a big piston.

A great deal of the land in the area of the ranch was owned by the State. Much of it was barren prairie land that was hilly and full of crevices and gullies. Nothing much grew on it except sage brush and patches of scrub oak. The State worked out a plan that involved the Bureau of Land Management whereby the land was surveyed and staked and then the large earth moving scrapers that were pulled behind Caterpillar tractors moved the dirt to make level fields. At that time, the penitentiary was paid seven cents for every cubic yard of dirt that was moved to make land that could be irrigated and suitable for growing crops. I learned to read grade stakes. The stakes were marked with a 'C' or an 'F' which designated if it was a cut or a fill. The number accompanying the C or the F on each stake was in tenths of feet. If a stake read F/5, it meant that the area near that stake needed to be filled six inches or a half foot.

When it was time to move one of the cats from one field to another field that might be a mile or so down the road, we always went in reverse. Bulldozers are slow and powerful going forward, but the gear ratio allows them to go faster when backing up.

Working on a Caterpillar tractor all day was dusty and dirty hard work. Some days I was covered with dirt from head to toe. A hot shower, some clean clothes and a warm supper made it all better. One of the benefits of my job was that I didn't have time to feel sorry for myself. I didn't dwell on the fact that I was in prison. The days passed quickly and when it was time for lights out, I went right to sleep every night. I got along well with the other men who lived in the tractor barn. As far as being locked up is concerned, I think I had it about as good as anyone, and I had learned to be a "Cat skinner."

We were allowed visits only on the weekends. When I was lucky enough to get a visit, I was taken by truck to Medium Security about two miles from the ranch where there was supervised visitation.

SUBPOENA

I had been at the ranch a couple of months, and I thought things were beginning to look a little better for me when in December, 1961, I was subpoenaed to return to Denver. I was to testify against other police officers who had been arrested and charged in the ongoing police investigation. I had no option. This was not a good thing. It was difficult enough for me as an ex-police officer doing time in the state penitentiary. I was already suspected of being a snitch by much of the population. I thought, "Why can't they just leave me alone and let me do my time?" If I go back to Denver and take the stand to testify against my former fellow officers, I would be sealing my own fate. I believe the other inmates would have cut my throat as soon as I got back to the prison.

I was transported from the state penitentiary to the Denver County jail to wait being taken downtown to the Denver District Court to testify.

The district attorney had several cases, and I was scheduled to be the star witness. When it was time for the first case, I was shackled and taken to court. The case involved former police officer Jack Snodgrass. I admitted knowing Jack and being with him on a particular night. I had no choice; it was a matter of record in the police log book. During my testimony I feigned memory loss and was vague about details, but there were other witnesses, and Jack was convicted. I felt bad for Jack and myself. The fact that I had taken the witness stand and Jack was convicted gave me the label of "rat."

Not long after that, the sheriff's office sent for me again. By now I had made up my mind that I was not going to be a witness. What was the point? I had already been sentenced. There was no advantage for me to testify; it could only cause me further grief and pain. When I took the stand the prosecutor asked me to state my name for the record.

"Arthur Winstanley," I said.

"And where do you live?"

"I'm an inmate at the Colorado State Penitentiary."

"Mr. Winstanley, do you recognize the defendant in this case?"

"I refuse to testify."

"What do you mean you refuse to testify?"

I became a bit emotional, my voice cracked as I blurted out, "I'm not going to help you any more now or ever. I'd rather be a live convict than a dead rat."

The district attorney was angry. "Well if you refuse to testify, I'll ask that you be found in contempt," he shouted.

The judge then said to me, "Do you understand that if you refuse to testify and are found in contempt of this court that I can sentence you to the county jail?"

I sat still for a moment. I thought to myself. "I'm doing 4 to 8 years in the state penitentiary, and this guy is threatening me with being sent to the county jail."

"Well, your Honor," I said, "I believe I'll take it."

"You'll what?" the judge said.

Then, before anyone spoke, a man stood up in the crowded court room and said, "The court will recognize me as a member of the bar, and if this witness is to be charged, he should have the right to counsel. If it pleases the court Your Honor, I'll advise this witness." The man was Anthony (Tony) Zarlengo, a well known criminal attorney in the Denver area.

The judge then pointed his gavel at the man and said. "All right, sir, you've got the job."

Mr. Zarlengo came forward and said, "Your Honor, I'd like to ask for a short recess while I confer with my client."

"Ten minutes," the judge said.

Mr. Zarlengo and I went into an adjacent room and sat down at a small table. I told him that nothing the court could do to me would be worse that what would happen if I were to testify. He said, "Then don't." When we went back into the courtroom, I got back on the witness stand. The prosecutor then said, "I'll ask you again, Mr. Winstanley, do you know the defendant in the case?"

"I've been advised by my council that I don't have to talk to you people." I said.

There was some discussion at the bench between the district attorney, Mr. Zarlengo and the judge. I could not hear what was said, but when they stepped away, the prosecutor said, "This witness is excused."

The ex-police officer whom I was scheduled to testify against in this matter was acquitted, but later found guilty in some other burglaries.

A few days later the Sheriff's department transported me back to Canon City from the Denver County jail. I was immediately processed in the main prison and sent back out to the Ranch. It was nice to be home.

THE MAGICAL EVENING

Almost overnight I realized that it was springtime. It was April, 1962. I have always thought that the best Colorado has to offer is in the spring. I had been at the Ranch for six months.

The Canon City area of Colorado is a beautiful part of the state. The air is always crisp and clean. The majestic snow capped mountains of the Sangre de Cristo range can be seen a few miles to the southwest.

I wandered out after supper one evening. We did not have to be in the dorm for "count" until 9:00 p.m. I walked down the road a short distance and sat on the rail fence. It was a strange sensation to be able to walk freely in the open air with no bars or razor wire. An inmate could walk away, and occasionally one would, but that was something I never considered. My picture had been in the news so much the past year that someone would surely recognize me and I knew I wouldn't get far. Besides, I had no place to go but home. That was the only place I wanted to be.

As I sat there on the fence, even though I was in prison, I have rarely felt such freedom of soul and sprit. In the perfect quiet of the evening, I could hear the gentle rustling of the leaves as the evening breeze drifted through the giant cottonwood trees. I could hear the distant call of the mourning doves. I could smell the freshness of the alfalfa in the fields. I was overcome with a wonderful feeling that I knew I could never duplicate. I realized it was probably a once-in-a-lifetime experience. A feeling of total contentment and inner warmth seemed to fill my body from my nose to the tip of my toes and throughout my soul. The world seemed totally at peace for me at that time. As I walked back along the dirt road to the bunk house I could hear the crickets and the locusts. What I experienced that evening has always left a warm spot in my heart for the chirping of crickets in the evening, and the calling of mourning doves.

I adopted the attitude that if I had to be in prison, this was about as good as it got. I was determined to make the best of it and do as well as I could. This attitude served me well, but I felt I didn't have any other reasonable choice.

MEDIUM SECURITY

The Medium Security facility had been operational for about a year when I arrived at the Ranch. It was mostly built using convict labor, and many of the inmates who were housed there had worked on the construction. It was a very large facility that covered what would be the equivalent of 3 or 4 city blocks. It was totally enclosed with an 8-foot fence. There were 300 or 400 inmates assigned there. It was about eight miles from the main prison in Canon City. Some of the inmates lived in a dormitory part of the facility. Others lived in individual cells. Security was not as rigid as in the main prison because the type of inmates who were assigned there were non-violent offenders and usually were within a couple of years of their release date.

In addition to going to the Medium Security facility for our visits, everyone from the Ranch who wanted to go to the commissary to purchase personal items jumped on a flat bed truck on Saturday mornings for transport to the canteen at Medium Security. If there was money in your prison account there were many items to spend it on in the canteen. There were the necessary items like toothpaste and razor blades or luxury items such as ice cream and candy.

The razor blades that we were able to purchase were standard safety blades. There was not the concern at medium security over using them as weapons as there was in the main prison. Razors were kept by the guards in the main prison and inmates were watched carefully while using them. At one point while I was inside the walls, I had an electric razor. It was a Remington, with four cutting surfaces. One night I was using the electric razor on my stubble when it was "lights out." When the power was turned off, the whiskers that were only partially cut were caught between the screen and the blade in the razor. The damn razor just hung there stuck on my face. I couldn't get off, and it hurt. I thought I would yell for the guard to turn the lights back on for just a minute. Yeah right, like that might work. I finally managed to disassemble the cutting part and get it loose.

The most important item to purchase at the canteen was cigarettes. Cigarettes were used as the coin of the realm as it were. Cigarettes were used as exchange between inmates for nearly everything. This included giving the barber a pack to get a decent haircut or buying some new socks from an inmate who had extras sent from home by his dear old mother. I usually had plenty of cigarettes (and plenty of socks) because I ran a small poker game in the evenings and on the weekends. There were no chips. We played for cigarettes.

By the spring of 1962, all of the policemen who were charged and convicted as a result of the police scandal were doing time. The total was 45. Nearly every officer who was in any way connected to any police burglary or implicated in police corruption or theft was sent to prison. There were a few who did not go to jail but were dismissed from the force. These officers who were spared had limited knowledge of wrongdoing and did not participate in any theft.

Policemen are held to a higher standard, as well they should be. Normally a person who is guilty of burglary might get probation if he has no record or past history of criminal activity. Police officers, however, can not stand up and take an oath to uphold all the laws and vow to serve the people and then get caught with their hand in the cookie jar and expect to be treated with leniency.

There were two or three ex-policemen sent to the Ranch, but the majority of them were assigned to Medium Security. By late summer of 1962 there were enough ex-policeman at Medium Security that they formed their own softball team. They called their team "The Cops and Robbers." The softball games promoted a healthy and spirited rivalry between the cops and other inmate teams.

I would often see other former police officers in the visiting room at Medium Security on the weekends. Occasionally we were allowed to ride in a truck to Medium Security on the weekends for one of the softball games where I had a chance to talk to some of the ex-cops. The words of our conversations were guarded and very casual. I think that no one was real sure about who had said what about whom and no one wanted to talk about why they were there.

Many of the inmates who lived at Medium Security worked outside the facility during the day. For the most part they worked along the roads doing maintenance, picking up trash or cutting weeds.

When the need for extra help arose at the Ranch, it came from Medium Security. Details of men were sent as needed when it was harvest time in the orchards or time to pick the corn or dig potatoes. Two or three times each summer when it was time to cut the alfalfa and bale the hay we got extra help from the men at Medium Security.

NEWS FROM HOME

Working outside on a Caterpillar tractor during the winter months in Colorado can often be cold and miserable. Wednesday, January 24, 1962, started like most other days. It was not as cold as some, but there was a biting wind out of the north. At the end of the work day in the field, I was anxious to get back inside where it was warm. I took a hot shower, and as I sat on my bunk waiting for the big bell outside the kitchen door to sound supper time, Tony, the evening guard, came to me and said, "Come to the office after supper, I'll take you to Midway. Captain Tipton wants to talk to you."

"All right, sir, I'll be there," I said. I knew that this was not good news.

Midway was a small office building just across the road from Medium Security. This building served as the administration offices for all of the outside facilities. It was headquarters for Captain Clarence (Wine Belly) Tipton who was in charge. If an inmate was summoned to this building because Captain Tipton wanted to talk with him, it was never a good thing.

169

It meant that you were being served with divorce papers or that someone in your family had been seriously injured, or passed away, or even worse, had been killed.

I could not eat my supper. Every inmate had to go to the chow hall and sit in his assigned seat until the count was clear. The chow hall was where everyone was counted at each meal. As soon as the guard saw that everyone was present and accounted for and had indicated the count was clear, I left to go sit on my bunk and wonder why I was being asked to go to the main office. My mind raced as I contemplated all that could be wrong. What had happened? Had one of my children been kidnapped, or even killed? Had my wife been in a terrible accident? Someone surely must have died; why else would the captain send for me?

It seemed like a long time before supper was over and the guard came out. Again I waited while Tony did some paper work. After a while he motioned me to come with him. We both got in the old green prison pickup and started toward Captain Tipton's office. Tony knew what I was going to be told, but it was not for him to say. Neither of us spoke. When we pulled up in front of the building, I could see a light on in the front office. I got out and walked in. Tony waited in the truck.

As I walked in, I could see Captain Tipton at his desk. He glanced up at me as I walked in and indicated for me to sit in one of the chairs across from his desk.

"I've got some bad news, Art," he said. "Your father died." Even though I suspected this was the reason I had been called to his office, it was a shock to hear the words.

The reason that each inmate is personally summoned to the captain's office for any type of disturbing news is so that the captain can gauge his reaction. The concern is that an inmate might be so distraught after getting some terrible news that he might feel the need to escape. It would be easy for an inmate to walk away from any of the outside prison facilities if he was terribly upset over some personal problems. If the captain felt that an inmate was upset to the point that he might do something foolish, like escape, the inmate was immediately sent to Medium Security to be held in a cell until it was further determined how he was going to adjust to the news.

Of course, I knew all of this. I knew that the captain was looking at me closely so that he could monitor my reaction. I also knew that how I reacted to this news was going to determine where I slept that night. I did not want to appear so upset that the Captain would send me inside the walls right then and there.

I also knew that in some cases trusted inmates had been allowed to attend family funerals if the captain approved. The inmate had to have sufficient funds in his account to hire a guard to accompany him, and pay other expenses such as gas and mileage for the guard's personal vehicle.

All of this was going through my head as the captain told me that my mother had called the warden earlier in the day to say that my father, who had not been very well, had died rather suddenly at home.

Actually, I thought this was about the best bad news I could have heard. I did not like my father. He was a selfish drunk, always thinking of himself first. He was not kind to my mother. I thought that if anyone in my family had to die, better it be him.

I had to be very careful about how I acted and what I said if I was going to convince the captain that I was remorseful but that I could handle this news and still be in complete control of my emotions. If I told the captain that I did not like my father, I might ruin my chances of going home for the funeral. I wanted to appear as adult and mature as possible. I looked the captain in the eye and said, "This is not totally unexpected. I thought this might be why you sent for me. My father was a good man, and that's the way I'll remember him." I then added, "I feel sorry for my mother, but she is a strong woman and I know she can get through this."

I asked the captain if I could get permission to call home. He told me that I could not call then, but that it could be arranged for me to call in the morning.

I stood up and shook hands with the captain. I told him that I would fill out a phone call permission slip and bring it back in the morning after breakfast. I walked out of his office and out to the truck where Tony was waiting. I told Tony that my father had passed away, which he already knew. I repeated nearly the same words to Tony as I had said to the captain, not wanting to give him any indication that I was upset or that I might be considering "running off."

The news of my father's death resulted in a restless night. Mixed feelings about my father kept me awake. My dad was an alcoholic and a terrible role model. He was mean to me and my brothers and inconsiderate to my mother. He demanded obedience without question in matters that I felt were unimportant while more important issues such as religion, money, morality and character were never discussed. I tossed and turned during the night. He was my father. He gave me life, and on some level he must have loved me, but I hated him.

I filled out the required phone call request form, and after breakfast, I caught a shuttle ride back to the captain's office. The reason the captain had not allowed me to call the night before was that the administrative staff had gone for the day, and all phone calls were monitored. I was able to call home and talk with my mother. Again I was mindful that our conversation was being monitored and chose my words carefully. I told my mom that I loved her very much, and that I had always admired her strong faith in God. I assured her that I knew she was a strong lady and that her faith would help give her direction and courage. She said the services were planned for Saturday, and asked if there were any way I could get permission to come home for the funeral. I explained that I would have to get permission from the captain and be able to show that I had sufficient funds in my account to compensate a guard and pay expenses for the trip to Denver. She offered to send me any money that I might need if I could just come home for the day. I thought I had enough money in my account to cover all the costs, but I was glad that the guard who was listening heard the conversation.

After we hung up, I asked to speak with the captain. As I waited my turn to talk with the captain, I went over in my mind what I should say to help convince him to let me go home on Saturday. After a short time, the captain asked me to come in. I pleaded with him to allow me to go home on Saturday for my father's funeral. He said he would look into the matter, and get word back to me through the guard at the Ranch by afternoon. I think he needed to get an OK from the warden or associate warden, and check my inmate account for funds and perhaps see if there was a off duty guard willing to escort me to the service.

The good news came right after lunch, when the guard at the Ranch informed me that I had been given permission to attend my father's funeral on Saturday. I was permitted another phone call to inform my mother that I would be coming home for the funeral. She cried, and said she would be waiting for me.

THE FUNERAL

The guard went over a list of things that I would be required to do before making the trip home. First I made out a prison cash transfer slip from my inmate account to cover the estimated cost of the guards salary and other expenses. Next, I was told that I had to catch the shuttle bus Friday morning and go to the main prison in Canon City for "dress out."

Of course I was ready and waiting when it was time to catch the bus. Going back inside the walls was a hassle. It meant going through the west gate for a thorough strip search, which was always a degrading and humiliating experience. I had bad memories of being behind the walls of the main prison, and for me it was frightening and depressing.

After passing through the west gate, a guard escorted me to the dressing room near the tailor shop where an inmate measured me for a suit of clothes. Going in for "dress out" was the same procedure as inmates go through the day before they are released from prison either on parole or discharge. Racks of new clothes, made in the prison tailor shop, in many different sizes, lined the walls of the dressing room. After I was measured, the inmate told me which racks contained clothes in my size. An inmate could choose a suit or a pair of dress pants and a coat if he wished. There was also a large selection of shirts and ties as well as shoes. I tried some things on and made a selection. Each inmate was allowed to choose an outfit upon his release. I don't know what it is about prison clothes, but there is nothing that looks more like a prison suit than a prison suit.

All of the clothes I had selected were put in a box, and the guard carried the box as he escorted me back to the west gate to wait for the bus that would take me back to the Ranch. The box of "street clothes" were kept in the possession of a guard or locked up until it was time for me to get dressed for the funeral to prevent them from falling into the hands of some unauthorized person who might try to use them to escape.

When I arrived back at the Ranch, I was informed that Lieutenant John Chesley would be at the Ranch at eight the next morning to escort me to Denver. I had heard that Lieutenant Chesley was a real hard nose, and a stickler for the rules. There were many guards that I would have preferred to accompany me, but of course, I had no choice.

On Saturday morning, after I showered and shaved, I went to the office where I got dressed in the clothes I had picked out and sat down to wait for the Lieutenant to arrive. When Lieutenant Chesley arrived at the Ranch, we were introduced and he signed me out. As we walked out to his car, I was impressed at how nice he looked. His hair was graying. I would guess he was in his fifties. He appeared rather distinguished wearing a well tailored business suit. The car he drove was a clean and well cared for 1958 Chevrolet Impala. We made small talk about a lot of insignificant things as we drove toward my mother's home in south Denver. I was comforted by the fact that he seemed so at ease as we drove along the highway. He smiled easily, and did not seem to fit the impression that I had been given of him.

My mother must have been watching for us because when we pulled up in front of the house and got out, she came out of the house to meet us. We shared an emotional embrace. Mother had tears in her eyes. She was extremely pleased that I was home, even if it was just for the day.

There have not been many days in my life that are as memorable as that Saturday. My wife and children were there as well as both of my brothers and their wives. Being able to put my arms around friends and family was very special. My wife had put out some clothes and my suit because she did not know what I might be wearing. I asked Lieutenant Chesley if I could change into my own suit, and he said that would be fine. This allowed me to have a little private time with my wife in the back bedroom when I changed clothes and again later in the day when I changed back into the prison suit that I wore home.

The service for my father was very nice. The gathering of family and friends and the freedom of being there made it a special day for me. After the service there was a reception at my mother's home with an abundance of food and desserts provided by neighbors and friends. There were forty or fifty people at the house during the reception. Everyone knew that I was doing time in the state penitentiary yet no one ever mentioned a word about how I was able to be there to attend the funeral, at least not to me.

Lieutenant Chesley was never far away. Occasionally I would see him chatting with people and drinking coffee, but he blended in so well that I don't think anyone knew who he was or why he was there. I could not have chosen a better person to accompany me home.

After most of the guests had gone I looked at Lieutenant Chesley and knew it was time for us to start back to Canon City. Amid some tears, I said all my goodbyes and held my mother before leaving. It was a nice drive back. I had a wonderful warm feeling about the day.

It was dark when we arrived back at the Ranch. I expressed my gratitude to Mr. Chesley for all he had done. I went to the officers' quarters to change my clothes again and turn in my prison suit for my regular prison blues. Later that night I laid in my bunk in the still of the darkness remembering the awesome events of the day.

When I was a little boy, about eleven or twelve, during the summer I would fish for crappie in front of the boat house at Washington Park. There were two old men that often sat on the bench near the dock where I fished. I overheard their conversation one day when they were discussing if there was anything in the world that was worth whatever you had to pay for it. They weren't talking about fresh air or clean water; it was about things you had to pay for. One of the old men thought it was a successful pheasant hunting trip or a good trout stream. The other said he believed it was a good haircut or a comfortable pair of shoes.

I don't remember what I paid for my trip home that January day, but it brought a smile to my face to think about how much bang I got for my buck the day we buried my daddy.

PAROLE AND DIVORCE

SENTENCE CUT SHORT

The sentencing structure varies in each jurisdiction and each state. The amount of time a prisoner actually serves per year of sentence also varies. I don't know of any two states that are alike. The federal correctional system is also different. Federal prisoners serve more time per year of their sentences, but federal prisons are usually nicer facilities with better accommodations. You might want to check all this out before you decide to rob a bank.

I had been sentenced to a term of 4 to 8 years, which meant I was eligible for a parole after serving the "minimum" on a 4-year sentence. The minimum on a 4 year term at that time was 27-7 (27months and 7 days.) The "minimum" is a calculation of earned good behavior time, statutory good time, and the warden's trustee good time.

Legislative bodies throughout the country determine the amount of good time that can be earned as a means of control over the inmates. This allows some incentive for the prisoner to comply with the rules set forth in jails and prisons. It also frees up badly needed space, because most of the jails in this country are crowded to overflowing.

In addition, at that time, an inmate could elect to give blood every six weeks in exchange for $5.00 to be added to his account, or an additional 5 days off his sentence. For me it was a no-brainer. I took the days instead of the dollars. Surprisingly, most of the inmates who gave blood took the money. I thought that was crazy, but many of the prisoners did not have family or friends who could send them money.

In January 1963, totally out of the blue, Governor Steven L. R. McNichols commuted my sentence to "time served." I had been in prison for nearly two years. With all of my good time intact and the blood time, I was scheduled for parole in April. The commute came when I only had about 90 days left to serve. I never knew what prompted the Governor to commute my sentence, or what force might have been in place at the time. I had been the first policeman arrested and was, of course, responsible for the initial investigation that led to the police scandal. I also had received a longer sentence than most of the policemen who followed me. Whatever the reason, it seemed to me to be such a wonderful thing but it was of little help. If the Governor had intended to commute my sentence, why had he not done it sooner? As it turned out, it was somewhat of a mixed blessing.

It took about three days to process the paperwork, but I dressed out (was issued a suit of clothes and a pair of black military shoes). I was given the obligatory $25.00 and escorted to the front gate. The old timers say, "When you walk out the gate, never look back." Even though I was being released early, I would still have the remainder of my original sentence to do on parole.

My wife Eleanor was there to pick me up in the same '53 Chevrolet that the safe had fallen from in April, 1960. She drove. My license had expired, and I now would need the permission of the parole department to operate a motor vehicle. As we made the long drive back to Denver from the prison in Canon City, I thought about what freedom meant. I thought about the closeness and the smell of a woman and making love. I thought about having a cold beer and eating in a restaurant. I worried about trying to find a job to support my family. I felt the joy of being out of jail and the shame of having been there.

Within hours of my release I began to realize that things were not right. My early release had caught Eleanor off guard. She didn't have time to get her "personal affairs" in order. I soon learned that during my absence she had many "friends." She had found somebody new. Within a week she confessed that she didn't love me anymore. Her words stopped the world from turning. I was devastated. I thought I had enough love for both of us, but it doesn't work that way. How could she put me down for some other guy? The emotions of anger, resentment and love were all mixed up. I had no job and no money. I took everything I owned in a couple of boxes and went to live with my mother. Everything was all wrong.

This was not at all what I had hoped for. I told my mom that I was happier when I was in jail. Eleanor had broken my heart. Sometime it takes more strength to let go than to hang on.

During my two years of incarceration I had dreamed of starting over when I was released. I had high hopes and plans to get my life on track. I wanted the chance to prove I could be a good father and husband. After the fish tank of cell house four and being sent to general population, I vowed that I would never cry again. – Oh, how I lied.

THE TAX MAN COMETH

My release was news in both of the Denver papers. I had been home about a week when a man from the IRS called. He said the IRS had three years to challenge a return. He explained that my income tax return for 1960 -1961 was being questioned and that the statute of limitations was about to expire. He asked if I would come down to his office and sign a waiver that would extend the limitations until he had a chance to look into my case.

After I was sure I understood what it was he was asking me to do, I made some reference to his ancestry and about some of his body orifices and told him some specific things about his mother before I hung up. A few days later I was served. The judgment was for several thousand dollars plus interest on money the IRS claimed I had stolen and not claimed as income on my return. The real glitch in this was that for insurance purposes the victims of a burglary in nearly every instance claimed losses far greater than the amount actually taken. I was being asked to pay income tax on the amount reported to the insurance company—not the nickel and a quarter that I had actually taken.

I went to see Burt Keating, who was the Denver District Attorney during the police scandal, and explained that the amount the government was asking me to pay was not realistic. He knew that the reported amount taken from many victims was inflated. However, the bottom line was that these were business owners in good standing, doing business with reputable insurance companies, and what an ex-convict had to say two or three years later was not going to convince anyone to change their minds about anything.

I met with the people from IRS several times to try to work something out. We did finally reach an agreement for about two thousand dollars. They set me up on a payment schedule that was nearly impossible to meet. When you owe the IRS money and they have a judgment against you there is not much wiggle room. They will garnishee your wages and put liens on just about anything you have. I felt that I would have received a better deal from the Mafia. I ultimately borrowed the money from my mother and paid the IRS.

After I had been home a few weeks, I got permission from my parole office to drive. I had my driver's license renewed and bought an inexpensive used car. It was then that I noticed something unusual. I was being followed by the Denver police. Detectives in unmarked cars were watching my every move day and night. I first thought they were detectives from the burglary division, but later decided they were from the intelligence bureau. What were they expecting to see? Did they expect to find some association with police officers that were still on the job? Did they suspect some conspiracy with other known felons? Some of the detectives followed along right behind me making no effort to conceal themselves. I suspect they were not thrilled with the assignment or that they wanted me to know I was being tailed. Why else would they make themselves so obvious? I don't know how long after my release this surveillance began before I noticed it, but after a few weeks it abruptly stopped.

FINDING A JOB

I had been out of prison for three weeks. My parole officer had given me permission to drive. I was growing impatient with living with my mother and not working.

I had entertained the idea of finding work as a bulldozer operator, and had contacted several large construction companies in the Denver area. There were no openings at the time. A few of them said they would take my application, but they were looking for heavy equipment operators for all types of heavy equipment. They needed people that were familiar with front end loaders, back hoes and other equipment as well as bulldozers.

About this time, I heard that the owners of a local chain of flower shops were looking for someone who was familiar with the Denver area to help with deliveries.

I went to see the folks at the flower shop. I told them who I was and where I'd been and that I was looking for a job. They hired me right then. I was very familiar with the Denver area. I knew all the streets. This knowledge was a result of my experiences as a police officer and a taxi driver and also due to the fact that I was a Denver native. I drove a delivery truck and during the holidays and busy times I was in charge of all the deliveries and routing other part-time drivers.

The Avenue Flower Shop was owned and operated by Clif and Mary Karstedt. They had several flower shops in the Denver area. Clif and Mary were down to earth, honest and decent people. They had no children. The flower shops were their family. Clif handled all the bookkeeping, billing, payroll and office business. Mary was the designer and she was in charge of flowers and supplies. She was an artist in the arrangement of flowers and very well respected in the flower business community.

Working at the flower shop was pleasant enough, but I was not happy. My biggest burden was self pity. I was angry at my wife, society, and the system in general. I felt that I had been given a raw deal by just about everyone. My bitterness and anger was misdirected. Evenings were spent at the local bar hanging out with other losers complaining about how badly I had been treated. I regularly drank myself into oblivion.

By now many of the other officers that had been involved in the police scandal had done their time and been released. Many moved away to make a new beginning. A man in the parole department told me that a couple of the ex-policeman had even changed their names. I gave some thought to leaving Denver. Perhaps if I moved far enough away people would not know me and I could make a fresh start. It was a tempting idea. I thought about going to Phoenix or back east. On the other hand, my mother was not well and I entertained the thought that perhaps my wife Eleanor would change her mind and take me back. I did nothing but continue to drink and feel sorry for myself.

In February, 1965, after suffering a brain aneurysm, my mother died. I hated God and everything he created. I felt my world was crumbling into ashes all around me. I had nothing to live for and nothing to hold on to.

The same week my mother died, a woman I had dated came to me and said she was pregnant. Aleen was a member of our Monday night bowling league sponsored by the Campus Lounge. There was no question that I was the father. We ran off to a Justice of the Peace in New Mexico and were married. For the most part, that's the way it was done in the sixties. We had little in common and after our son Ronald was born, we were divorced. It was an amicable divorce, and we remained good friends.

I can take no credit for the way any of my children were raised; I wasn't there. Remarkably, they all grew up to be well-adjusted responsible adults and are a source of immense pride to me.

After my mother passed away and another divorce, I felt more alone than ever. I was lost. I was an emotional wreck. I was angry and bitter. Inside I was searching for something. The strongest emotion I felt could best be described as desperate. I was desperate for something, but I didn't know what. I was not even aware that I was lost in the search. I thought that booze was my friend, but liquor was playing a terribly deceiving trick on me every day. Going to bed at night without a few drinks first was unthinkable.

My job at the flower shop was not very demanding, and because the owners wanted to help me and were such nice people, I managed to keep the job even though there were days when I was not of much help.

I began to notice that people were looking at me differently. The look in their eyes had changed from "how nice to see you" to one of disappointment and pity. Although I tried, there was not enough liquor to drown my bitterness.

During this period I chased a lot of women. I dated as many girls as I could and chased after every skirt I could find. I wanted to be needed. I don't remember how many or even their names, but there was one girl that was different from all the others. There was one girl who was somehow special. She was a Denver school teacher who worked at the flower shop during the summer and holiday times. She would later play a major role in my life. Her name is Thais.

HAPPY JACK & DANNY BOY

The house that my mother and I had lived in was now mine. The house had three bedrooms, so I decided to find a couple of roommates to help bring in some extra money. The two guys who I chose as renters were, of course, a couple of losers I knew from the Campus Lounge where I spent most of my spare time.

Jack had a pretty good job and always paid the rent on time. Danny, on the other hand, never had a dime. Danny didn't even have a car. It was up to Jack or to me to haul him around to wherever he thought he needed to be. Occasionally, I loaned him my car if he had a hot date or something. Jack's car was much nicer than mine, and I think Danny knew better than to ask to borrow his car. Danny was a good looking guy, and everybody seemed to like him, including me. I'm not sure just what the attraction was.

One Friday night at the bar, Happy Jack hooked up with a girl we called Fat Shirley. He brought her home to play honeymoon for the weekend. Monday morning, Jack was through with her, but Fat Shirley was in love.

192

For the next several months Fat Shirley chased after Happy Jack everywhere he went. I didn't care about her chasing after Jack. I was concerned, however, because she had four small kids ranging in age from about 4 to 9. She brought the kids out at night after they should have been in bed. I don't know where the kids were during the weekend she played house with Jack, but she had them with her every time I saw her after that. She would come into the bar looking for Jack at 9 or 10 p.m. I felt sorry for the kids (I called them "squids"). I would buy them all a soft drink and say "Why are you squids not at home in bed?" I would tell Shirley that if she couldn't find a baby sitter, she should stay home and not be dragging her squids out late at night. The kids always laughed when I call them squids. I'm telling you this story now because later on the kids show up in my life.

I felt sorry for Danny. He was such a likable guy but he was always down and out. He never seemed to have anything or catch a break. A couple of times he said to me that he wished I would teach him how to open a safe. I would laugh and tell him that was never going to happen, but it did.

After drinking far too much one evening we went to a small restaurant in east Denver. I'm not sure why we picked this place. I think Danny had worked there and said they had a safe in the back room. We crawled in through a small window in the rear of the restaurant and went inside. I was able to open the safe right away. We were in and out in less than 10 minutes. Danny was very impressed. For the next several days he repeatedly told me how skillful he thought I was. He said it was sure nice to work with a professional and that I must be the best safe cracker in the world. I ate it up. My starving self image was in need of some praise. The way Danny stroked my ego, I felt ten feet tall. The next few weeks the two of us were a crime spree. We were out of control. We were getting liquored up and burglarizing two or three places a week.

As any sane person might realize, we were destined for a fall. We were lacking the tools to be successful. We were handicapped because we had no back up, no police radio to alert us as to who was in the area or what calls they might be receiving, and no plan of what we might do in the event we were caught or surprised in the act. We were just two drunks having a good time at the expense of others.

In October of 1966, after closing, we drilled the safe in The El Capa Lounge on West 35th Avenue and Youngsfield in Wheat Ridge. We were spotted by a security guard, who notified the local police. We had no more than left the restaurant when we were arrested by the Wheat Ridge police and taken to the Jefferson County jail in Golden, Colorado. By the next day I had started to sober up and began to realize just how bad my situation was. I remember hearing myself say "Oh, God, what have I done?" How could I have done this after all that I had been through when I was in jail the first time. How in the world could I have been so stupid as to think I could get away with something like this? My thoughts were eerily the same as they had been six years earlier.

The detectives did not talk to me; they concentrated on Danny. They told him that he was going down big time if he did not cooperate with them. They told him that they knew these burglaries were not his idea, and that they were sure that being caught with a notorious burglar and safe cracker like Art Winstanley was just a bit of bad luck. The detectives told Danny he was going to prison for a long time unless he confessed. They also told him that he might even get probation if he came clean to everything. It worked. Danny was scared, and he started squealing like a pig. I was trapped. There was no way out. The best I could hope for was to make an apology, plead guilty and hope for leniency when it was time for sentencing. That did not work out very well either.

BACK TO PRISON

BACK TO THE JOINT

On Monday morning, December 5, 1966, Jefferson County District Judge Ronald Hardesty sentenced me to 7 to 10 years in the state penitentiary. My girlfriend, Thais, the only girl I really cared anything about, had driven me to the court house in Golden, and kissed me goodbye.

After sentencing, I was immediately remanded to the custody of the Jefferson County Sheriff's Department to await transportation to the state penitentiary at Canon City.

I felt very alone, but being sent back to prison was not nearly as frightening as it had been the first time. I knew what was in store for me, and what to expect. When I went to jail the first time I was bothered a great deal by the fact that my wife and family, particularly my mother and father, were suffering so terribly for what I had done. This time, my wife had divorced me and moved away. My children had a new daddy. My parents had both died.

When I was sentenced to prison the first time, I was dreading it so much I wished the time to go would never come. This time I wanted to hurry it up so I could start doing my time. I sat in the Jefferson County jail for four days before it was time to be taken to the prison. The time went by extremely slowly. I had the feeling I had been hit in the gut. I was sick about how I had gotten myself in such a huge mess. How could I have allowed this to happen? What could I have been thinking? I was so disappointed with myself I wanted to die.

On Thursday, the 8th of December, they came for me. I was shackled with leg irons and handcuffed to a body belt. The depression was so overwhelming I had to vomit. I knew that when I arrived at the prison the other inmates would be jeering me. I imagined what they would be saying, "Hooray, that rat bastard cop is back again."

It was going to be hard to listen to all their shouting and ridicule. It did not happen.

Just moments before I arrived at the prison, another new inmate was brought in who was a much bigger fish than I was, and he garnered all the attention. When I first saw the man being escorted in to the prison ahead of me by the Boulder county sheriff deputies, I had no idea who he was. He was a tall thin man about 38 years old. As he walked in front of me he was bent over and looked down. He seemed very meek and wispy as if you could knock him down with a feather. His name was Joe Morse. Joseph Dyre Morse had been convicted and sentenced to prison for 888 years for the rape and murder of Elaura Jeanne Jaquette.

The beautiful 20-year-old Colorado University student, whom friends and family called Lauri, was a zoology major. On a warm summer day in July, 1966 she was last seen eating her lunch on the lawn of the Boulder campus. It was later learned that she was lured up the 17 steps of the spiral staircase of the west tower of the Macky Auditorium at the Boulder campus. Several hours after she was last seen, two students walked up the staircase of the Macky Auditorium and found Jaquette's body in the organ recital room.

Blood was splattered across five of the six walls in the L-shaped room. Smudges of blood reached as high as seven feet above the wooden floor which was littered with broken glass and soaked in blood. Lauri Jaquette was raped and beaten to death. She had multiple fractures to the head and face. Several teeth were knocked out of her jaw. Cuts and bruises covered her neck, throat, and buttocks. Investigators who studied the room concluded she tried to crawl away from her attacker. The killer swung Jaquette by her feet.

After interviewing more than 1,500 people and four weeks after Jaquette's body was found, police arrested Morse who worked on campus as a janitor. He was held on suspicion of first-degree murder. The lead in the case came from Joe Morse's two teenage daughters who noticed him carrying a bucket of bloody clothes home on the day Jaquette was killed. A bloody palm print found on a piece of plywood near the murder scene matched Morse's hand.

Dave Voorhis, who was an investigator for the Boulder police department, said it was the most horrific and brutal crime scene he had ever seen. Dave Voorhis went on to be the chief of the Boulder Police Department.

The murder and rape of this young coed and the trial of Joe Morse had been covered extensively by the media in Colorado. A crime that was this heinous and brutal caught the attention of the inmates, and it seems they were all waiting to see this guy when he got to prison. Joseph Dyre Morse was issued number 37884. I was inmate number 37885.

Again I was assigned to cell house four. Every new inmate, whether he has been there before or not, does the mandatory four weeks in the fish tank for indoctrination and evaluation. The routine was the same: Hair cut, blood tests, physical examination, and learning the rules.

Joseph Morse was there too, but we did not talk. Joe was a loner. He was very quiet and kept totally to himself. Murderers are well accepted in prison society, rapists are not. Joe Morse did not get a lot of mail, I did. My girlfriend, Thais, the school teacher, wrote to me every day.

Morse maintained his innocence until 1980, nearly 15 years later, when he confessed to the crime. After serving nearly forty years, Joe Dyre Morse died in 2005, at age 77, according to the Colorado Department of Corrections.

THE WEEK BEFORE CHRISTMAS

There were about twenty inmates in the fish tank with me as the holiday season approached. Arrangements had been made for a chorus group of young people from a local school to come to the penitentiary on Sunday, December the 18th. They were to entertain the inmates with Christmas carols in the auditorium.

The purpose of the fish tank was to keep the new inmates separated from the general population until the orientation process was complete and the new inmates had an opportunity to adjust to being in prison. The prison administration made the decision that the inmates in the fish tank could attend the performance if they could be seated in a separate area where they would be isolated, and not allowed to mingle with the other inmates.

An area of seats was roped off on one side of the auditorium for the "fish." We were all pretty excited that we would be allowed to attend the Christmas show. The performance was outstanding. Even by the standards that one might expect on the outside, the young singers were exceptional.

Near the end of their performance, all of the young singers came on stage and sang, "I'll be home for Christmas if only in my dreams."

As the inmates stood to applaud, I looked around at the other convicts. I have never seen so many tears in the eyes of so many men at the same time in my life, including my own.

DR. LEVY

When it was time to leave the fish tank, and join the general population, I was transferred to cell house six. A guard escorted me so that I could be checked in. Of course I knew where cell house six was; I had lived there on my previous visit. The moment I stepped inside the door I recognized the smell. Penitentiary cell houses all have a distinct smell. It is not particularly bad, it was just unique. It is hard to describe, but like a dead body or burning flesh, once you have experienced that smell you never forget.

I was assigned to work in the mattress factory. It was just a job to keep me busy until a regular job assignment was available. The inmates who have graduated high school and particularly those of us who could type were usually assigned a better or at least a more prestigious job. After working in the mattress factory for less than two months I was given a new job that turned out to be a real doozy.

I was assigned to be the clerk for Dr. George Levy, the prison psychologist. Even before I was supposed to report for work on Monday morning, I heard that Dr. Levy was pretty far out there. Over the years, I have met some people who I thought were a little dingy, but after working as Dr. Levy's secretary for only a week, I concluded he was a genuine nut case.

He was a little round guy with receding hair and horn rimmed glasses. He wore a bow tie and a vest to work every day. All of his vests were the type that were seamed down the center in the back. These vests had been taken apart at the seam and stitched back together with a different vest. One day his vest was paisley on one side and plaid on the other. The next day it was polka dot on one side and striped on the other.

After working for him a few days, I summoned the courage to ask why he wore vests that were always so different. "Ah," he exclaimed, "it's to evoke questions that precipitate dialogue." I was tempted to say something like, "Hey, asshole, you're talking to your inmate clerk, not the chairman of the board."

As the prison psychologist, one of Dr. Levy's functions was to evaluate each prisoner within a reasonable amount of time after the prisoner arrived at the institution. Dr. Levy did not see each prisoner individually. In many cases he would look at the jacket or file of an inmate and make a preliminary diagnosis. I don't know why he bothered. I could have done what he did. Every inmate, without exception, was diagnosed with anti-social personality disorder and labeled "sociopath," including me. Perhaps Dr. Levy was correct in his diagnosis, but many of the inmates had much deeper problems.

Within the vast realm of mental illness lie several areas of disorder. I suspect that to some degree, everyone has occasional visits to one or another of these domains. This is not to imply that everyone has a chronic disorder, but simply that the difference between mentally ill and mentally well is a smaller margin than one might think.

Dr. Levy did see some inmates on a regular basis. For some reason he took a special interest in certain cases for study and would see these individuals at least once a week. I think he had his own agenda about what type of individual he considered in need of his counseling.

One of the inmates Dr. Levy took a particular interest in was Stan McClure. I'm not sure what his interest in Stan was, but it was totally one sided. Stan hated to go see Dr. Levy every week. It not only disrupted his regular routine, it made it particularly difficult because the other inmates were suspicious of why he went to talk to the shrink every week. I believe the other inmates thought he might be a snitch. They were paranoid, and thought Stan was telling Dr. Levy things about them.

Dr. Levy was fond of giving the Rorschach test (ink blots) and of asking what type of animal an inmate might like to be. One afternoon, Dr. Levy asked Stan to draw a picture of an animal that he would most like to be. Stan drew a bear. Dr. Levy looked at the picture and said, "Now tell me Stan, is he a happy bear or a sad bear?"

"Oh, he's a happy bear." Stan replied.

"And why is he such a happy bear," the Doctor asked.

"Because he minds his own fucking business that's why!"

The good doctor was also prone to outbursts of rage. He would scream, shout, and pound on his desk when something upset him. One morning after working for Dr. Levy less than two months, he threw one of his frequent fits. He started hollering and he kicked his waste basket across the office. He told me that I was incompetent. "You have no business being my clerk," he shouted.

I shouted back, "I don't want to be your fucking clerk. You can stick this miserable job in your fat little ass."

Dr. Levy immediately called Captain Yoe on the phone, and my little ass went to the hole.

SOLITARY CONFINEMENT

I was marched off to cell house three to solitary confinement. I was stripped of all my clothes and given a pair of coveralls and one wool blanket. I was then put in an isolation cell. I sat in the corner holding my blanket all night. It was cold. I drifted off to sleep two or three times during the night, but not for very long. There were some almost inhuman screeches and screams coming from other cells in the isolation unit.

The next morning I was taken out of my cell and directed to a chair near a desk at the end of the hall. A few minutes later, Captain Yoe and some other officers came in and sat down at the desk. I was there for my "disciplinary hearing." It took the officers two minutes to determine that I needed an "attitude adjustment" that would take three days in the hole, starting now.

Another officer escorted me back to the cell where I had spent the night. The cell was totally bare except for a one-piece steel toilet in the corner. There was no toilet paper. There was a concrete pallet along one wall to sleep on. The cell was a concrete box with a double thick steel door and no window. There was a dim light covered by heavy steel mesh in the ceiling. The light came on about seven in the morning and went out at nine each night. That was the only indication I had of passing time. This was my home for the next three days. It seemed like weeks. The good part was that I could have all I wanted to eat and drink – as long as it was spinach, bread and water.

There was a variety of infractions that can earn an inmate time in the hole, but the majority of inmates who wind up in the hole are there for fighting. Occasionally two inmates would get into a verbal battle called "the dozens." To be engaged in this war of "put downs" was referred to as being "put in the dozens." The idea is to say something demeaning to another inmate. The other inmate would then respond with some words of disrespect to the first inmate.

This contest of "slams" or "snaps" would get progressively more personal and malicious as it went until one inmate did not have a come back.

"The dozens" can be a harmless game of casual, good-natured verbal jabs. In its purest form, "the dozens" is part of a custom of verbal sparring of "woofing" and "signifying" intended to defuse a potentially violent situation. It did not work that way in prison. "The dozens" often lead to bitter and bloody violence between inmates. Reference is often made to "yo mamma." Fathers and sisters are also popular targets, as well as the person they are trying to insult. No holds are barred in talking about the size, intelligence, age, skin color, or sexual performance of the opponent's family:

Does yo mamma know you're a punk bitch?

When I get out I'm gonna do your mamma – again – in the ass!

Well at least my mamma don't do oral sex on mules like your mamma!

It goes on and on. You can only imagine how insulting and obscene it can become.

I did some research and according to "Wikipedia" the free encyclopedia I found on the Internet:

"The dozens" has its origins in the slave trade of New Orleans where deformed slaves – generally slaves punished with dismemberment for disobedience – were grouped in lots of a "cheap dozen" for sale to slave owners. For a black to be sold as part of the "dozens" was the lowest blow possible.

Some believe this form of verbal banter to be the prelude to modern day hip-hop and rap.

After my time in the hole was done I was sent back to cell house six. I thought it had been the longest three days of my life. I would later learn that doing three days in the hole was a piece of cake.

The other inmates in cell house six knew that I had been in the hole. The rumors were rampant about what I had done to get there. Most of them thought I had punched the good doctor out. However, they all knew that striking an officer or a civilian staff employee like Dr. Levy would get you a lot more time in the hole than three days.

I was reassigned and sent back to work in the mattress factory until another "position" that I might be suited for became available.

During my first incarceration in the state penitentiary I played by the rules. If an inmate was giving me a bad time, I called him out to go the ring. This time was different. Out of contempt for the other inmates and frustration with myself, I lashed out immediately if someone gave me any grief. A loud mouth asshole got on my case in the mattress factory and I smacked him right there. The guard was not aware of what happened until later. In the meantime I got into another fight after work on my way to the cell house. This was not a good day. Two guards took me back to solitary. By the time I had my disciplinary hearing in the morning, the staff knew I had been involved in two incidents in one day. It was determined that I would lose ten days of my good time, and do ten days in the hole.

The psychological effect of being in solitary confinement for a long time can be devastating. Ten days is not a long time compared to some of the sentences handed out, but it seemed like forever to me. The old timers say that being locked in a small cell does not a prison make. They say it's all in your head and you must put your mind in a different place in order to escape. I was never able to go to that place. Although my desire was great, I could not will my mind away. Recalling the memories of better times and places helped me cope with the long hours of nothingness, but the realization of knowing where I was did not leave my mind. By the screams I heard day and night, I became aware of some inmates, who being unable to cope, were in a long dark descent into madness in a chamber of horrors. To my knowledge, Dr. Levy, the prison shrink, never visited the isolation unit.

After three days of spinach, bread and water, each inmate in solitary was given regular meals for one day. Some human rights organization (bless their bleeding hearts) won a decision in the Supreme Court that ruled not having regular meals at least every forth day constituted cruel and unusual punishment.

My ten days finally came to an end. Although I had been permitted out of my cell twice to shower, each time the door was opened, the outside light seemed very bright compared to the dim light in solitary. When the guards opened my door and told me to come out I was not sure it was really true. I had lost track of how many days I had been in the hole. I was lead back to my regular cell in cell house six, and told that I would once again be assigned to stuff mattresses in the mattress factory during the day.

When I returned to my cell it was evident that my things had been disturbed. The guards would often take the opportunity to carefully go through an inmates belongings when he was away i.e., doing ten days in the hole. They were looking for any type of contraband including drawings or written material.

I don't think they removed anything from my stuff, but I did discover some unexpected and unwelcome visitors in my cell. During my absence, my mattress had become home to an extended family of bed bugs. I first noticed that I had a string of 5 or 6 small red bites on my arm. The next morning, I discovered a line of similar red bites on my leg.

Bed bugs are a reddish brown insect usually about the size of a lady bug, (3/16 in. long). They are wingless and very flat. They usually live in bedding or upholstered furniture. The bugs come out at night and feed in a line along a blood vein.

The cell house had some bug spray that we could use in an attempt to get rid of the little critters, but it was not very effective because the bugs were so flat they got under the buttons on the mattress and were deep inside. It seemed that the bed bugs had taken up residence in just about every mattress in the entire cell house, and the bug spray was not doing much to curb the problem.

We came up with a plan that worked very well – we cooked 'em. In the prison tag plant, where the license plates and street signs were produced, there were huge ovens for baking on enamel paint. We signed up by putting our number on a list. Then on Saturday when the tag plant was not up and running, we would carry our mattress over to the plant and bake it in one of the big ovens for about an hour. It worked. The little critters couldn't take the heat. This along with the bug spray eventually got rid of the nasty little bed bugs.

COLSTIN

It was a while before another job opportunity came my way. COLSTIN was an acronym for Colorado State Industries. The program was set up in an effort to offset the cost of running the prison system and provide work for inmates. Under the COLSTIN name, the prison produced everything from furniture and clothing to canned food and dairy products. Mr. Al Urie was in charge of the program. He was the Superintendent of Industries. When his clerk/secretary was given a parole, I was assigned to Mr. Urie.

All of the products that were produced were sold and distributed to other state institutions in Colorado. Among the consumers were the state hospital at Pueblo, the state reformatory at Buena Vista, the Colorado School for the Deaf and Blind, and several public school districts.

Al Urie was a large robust man who was always pushing for more production at every level of the industries program. The inmates sarcastically referred to him as "Big Al, the convicts' pal."

When an inmate was granted a parole or discharged from the penitentiary he was issued a suit of clothes made in the prison tailor shop. The inmates referred to this as getting all dressed out in a new suit made by Hart Shafner and Colstin. (Hart Shafner and Marx was a well known men's clothing company at the time.)

As part of my duties in the office I made coffee, filed correspondence, and typed two or three letters each day. Copies were made using carbon paper. This was long before home computers were available. Even when Mr. Urie was out of the office, I was not allowed to answer the phone.

Nearly every letter I typed for Mr. Urie started out exactly the same:

"Dear _____,

"Owing to circumstances beyond which I have any control,"

The office for Colstin Industries was in the administration building which was centrally located inside the prison walls. The large three story building contained several business offices vital to the institution as well as the offices of the warden and the associate warden.

During the first few months I worked for Mr. Urie, I had difficulty locating papers from the files because there seemed to be no rhyme or reason to the filing system. I asked Mr.

Urie to requisition some file folders and I began the task of setting up a new filing system.

When Mr. Urie needed to talk to a client or a customer of any of the COLSTIN products he would simply pick up the phone and ask the operator to connect him with that business or the school he wanted. The phone operator was a female inmate who was brought to the main prison each morning where there was an area set up for the switchboard. The operator would look up the phone number of any institution, business, or school and make the connection. The women's prison was about two blocks north of the main men's prison.

One morning, Mr. Urie announced that he was leaving for an appointment, and that he would be out of the office most of the day. I had a wonderful idea. Why not call my girl-friend, Thais, the school teacher in Denver. I practiced what I was going to say and picked up the phone. Trying my best to sound like Mr. Urie, I asked the operator to connect me with Gove Junior High school in Denver. It worked. The lady in the office at Gove said that Thais was in class but that she could take a message. I told her to say that Art had called to say "Hi," and that I was thinking about her. Wow, I thought I was so cool. Thais would really be surprised to get that message. The surprise was on me.

Clandestine photo smuggled out by me, taken by inmate Hayward Lawson, prison photographer fingerprint classification department.

The inmate phone operator had seen Mr. Urie leave the building, and had not seen him return. She notified the authorities that she suspected something fishy going on with the phone in Mr. Urie's office. Well, well, how about that! Can you guess what happened next? Being the great detectives that they were, it didn't take the authorities long to figure that one out. Captain Yoe and some other security folks came into the office and I was on my way back to solitary.

The discipline hearing was the next morning and a new precedent was set. I was sentenced to eight days in the hole. However, Mr. Urie intervened and explained that he could not get along without a clerk. He did not understand the filing system and he could not type. It was decided that I would do my eight days in the hole on Saturdays and Sundays for the next four weeks. I would work at my job as clerk for Mr. Urie during the week. The arrangement was agreeable with me, but it created some difficulties with the other inmates. The general population took this arrangement as special treatment or favoritism toward me. Nothing like this had ever been done before.

During the time I worked for Mr. Urie, I became acquainted with another inmate clerk who worked in the building. Ron Rutherford, inmate #29885, was one of the most incredible people I have met. We became friends. I thought he was extremely intelligent. (You don't meet many smart people in jail.) Ron was well educated and well read. One of his most remarkable assets was an ability to express himself with words. He had an uncanny gift to hold a reader's attention with his writing. I had the privilege of reading many of his letters. He had an ability to control the emotions of his reader. He could make you laugh out loud or weep. The sad part of this man's life was that his energy was always directed at trying to put something over on the other guy or to find a way to beat the system. He had some wonderful ideas, but they were all illegal. Had he been able to channel his talents and knowledge in a legitimate endeavor, he would have been a true success story.

I enjoyed Ron's company. We had some great discussions. Sometimes, however, he used drugs and I did not like to be around him when he was high. He was not the same person.

Ron came up with a rather ingenious and simple plan for smuggling drugs into the prison. He made a lot of money selling drugs and even took orders from special customers for their substance of choice. There were no leftovers or shrinkage in Ron's drug business. What he didn't sell, he consumed. I was too afraid to participate in his drug business. (Ron had brass Brazilians.) However, I knew about it, and watched as he scored his stash on several occasions as it floated by. Let me tell you how this worked…

TENNIS, ANYONE?

There was an irrigation ditch than ran through the middle of the prison from the south to the north. It passed in front of the administration building where there was a stone bridge. The ditch was lined on each side with large stone blocks. The ditch was about five feet wide and always had water running in it. I never saw the bottom. There was an opening at each end of the prison wall where the ditch flowed in and out. The hole was about the size of a small car. The wall opening was covered with large reinforced steel bars that ran up and down about three inches apart. Occasionally, after a heavy rain, debris would pile up against the bars on the outside on the upstream end. Men from the outside maintenance crew using large rakes would have to pull the debris free to keep the water from backing up. A few hundred yards upstream from the prison a bridge on US highway 50 passed over this irrigation ditch.

Ron had several friends on the outside. He managed to get money to them and they would buy drugs in the Denver area. Someone would drive to Canon City with the drugs every couple of weeks. The illegal drugs most prevalent at the time were marijuana, heroin, and cocaine. Ron's friends would carefully seal the drugs in small plastic bags and then push them through a slit they had cut in a tennis ball. At a pre-arranged time, they would drive along highway 50 and throw the tennis ball from the bridge into the ditch. The current would carry the floating ball down the ditch and into the prison. The diameter of a tennis ball is two and a half inches and it would come into the prison between the bars. Ron would sit along the bank of the ditch pretending to be reading a book or taking in the sunshine. He would pick the ball out of the ditch when it went floating by, sometimes using a short stick. As crazy as it sounds, it worked beautifully. If he were to be caught, which he never was, his story was going to be that he just picked up the floating ball, and had no idea what it contained.

One day I noticed that my friend Ron did not leave the administration building when it was time to go to lunch. Later I went to the office where he worked and found him just staring out the window. We sat down and began to talk. He was high on something. He really laid a shocker on me. He admitted to having killed his girlfriend. I knew his girlfriend had been murdered two or three years before he came to prison. (Ron was doing time for theft and bad checks.) I never thought he might be responsible for her death.

He admitted to me that he had killed her in a fit of rage, and left her body in her apartment in the Capitol Hill area of Denver. He then said that he had gone home to his own house and attempted to commit suicide by slashing his arms and wrists. A family member found him in time to get some help before he bled to death. I had noticed the scars before, and asked about them, but he only said he had once tried to kill himself.

He said he had been arrested and spent several days in jail as a suspect in his girlfriend's murder, but that the investigators could not gather enough evidence to file a case. He even mentioned the detectives' names who had investigated the case. I recognized their names.

I was troubled by the fact that he could even do something like that, let alone that, he would tell me all about it. More troubling than all was what should I do? I was uncomfortable that he had laid this on me. As serious as this was, I couldn't go to the authorities and give him up. I was his friend and I was in prison. What was I supposed to do? If I were to rat him out, I'd be signing my own death warrant.

I assured Ron that his secret was safe with me, but my association with him was somewhat cool after his confession. I was afraid that somehow the cops might find out that he was the killer, and he would think I gave him up.

Many years later I turned this information over to detective sergeant Ben Trujillo of the Denver Police Department cold case unit. Ron had passed away, but I thought the police department would like to clear this case. I don't know what if anything was done.

THE HOSPITAL

When I left the mattress factory and went to work for Mr. Urie, I put in for a transfer from cell house six to cell house one. I knew there was a waiting list and that it would take some time, but I had plenty of "time."

Cell house six was the oldest cell house still being used, and cell house one was the newest. Cell house one was much cleaner, brighter and the cells were much larger. In addition to that, the toilets were nicer. They had seats – some things are important.

After I had been on the waiting list for four months, I was informed that I could move if I would be willing to take a cell on "Cadillac row." I elected to take it.

Shortly after transferring to cell house one, I was seriously injured. During my first prison term, there were several attempts on my life, but I was never badly hurt. This time I was not so lucky. I did not become aware of many of the details surrounding this incident for several months.

It seems there was a close knit group of Latino prisoners in cell house one that objected to my living in "their" cell house. They considered my choosing to move there as "signifying disrespect" which they would not tolerate.

As I walked into the cell house one afternoon after "yard," I got the back of my head caved in. There was a small area just inside the doorway to the cell house where you had to turn to get into the main building. Two men hid in the corner of this little entrance area with a large piece of jagged concrete. As I came through the first door, and started to turn, they hit me from behind. In keeping with the prison code, no one saw anything or knew anything about what happened. The blow knocked me to the floor of the cell house. I was only unconscious for a minute or two before I realized I was lying in a pool of my own blood. I staggered to my feet and started back out of the cell house toward the prison hospital. A guard came to my assistance and held a handkerchief to the back of my head as we made our way to the hospital. Blood ran down my back and covered my shirt.

I slipped in and out of consciousness for the next hour or two and don't recall all the details clearly. A black inmate by the name of Hill who worked in the prison hospital sewed the back of my head up with twenty-one stitches. I was not given anesthetic or anything for pain, because that could only be ordered by a licensed physician. The only real doctor for the prison who lived in Canon City had gone for the day. They did not call him back because the doctor's assistants, who were inmates with medical training, did not feel my injuries were life threatening. My shirt had been cut off and my pants removed. I was wearing a green hospital smock. The pain was so intense I became sick to my stomach. I was then helped down a long hall to the x-ray room.

The x-ray technician was inmate #33322. His name was Joe Corbett. He was another rather infamous inmate. Joseph Corbett, Jr., a former Fulbright scholar, became the 127th fugitive named on the FBI's Ten Most Wanted list. He was placed on the list on March 30, 1960, for the kidnap and murder of Adolph Coors lll, heir to the Coors Beer fortune. It was an extortion attempt that did not go as planned. A nationwide manhunt was conducted that spanned from California to Atlantic City, New Jersey, and eventually to Vancouver, British Columbia, Canada. Corbett was finally arrested October 29, 1960, in Vancouver by Canadian police after two Canadian citizens recognized him from a November, 1960, Reader's Digest article. Joe took x-rays of my head looking for evidence of a concussion. I was never told what the x-rays revealed. I don't know where Joe Corbett gained his knowledge of taking and reading x-rays, but he was very well respected in the field. Many health professionals thought he was the best x-ray technician in the state.

I remained in the hospital for the next two days. In the morning, I was seen by the doctor. He said that inmate Hill had done a nice job of stitching, which was of little comfort to me at the time because my head was throbbing with pain. The doctor left a prescription with the Lieutenant of the hospital. The prescription called for me to receive one cc of Demerol every 4 to 6 hours. I could hardly wait for the medication.

Finally an inmate nurse accompanied by a prison guard arrived with a syringe. The nurse took a small pinch of skin between his thumb and forefinger on the back of my arm and inserted the syringe. I experienced some psychological relief knowing the drug would soon take effect. It did not happen. The pain and throbbing did not subside. I was given another shot in the afternoon and another that evening. The result was the same. I was told that I would feel better soon.

I was released from the hospital on the second day with an envelope containing six aspirin and told to go back to my cell house.

It was several months later when an internal scandal involving the hospital workers revealed the truth. The inmates who worked as nurses in the hospital were all inmates who had some medical training. A few of them had actually been nurses, doctors' assistants, or paramedics on the outside. Strong pain killers and addictive drugs like Codeine, Morphine and Demerol were kept locked up by the prison guards assigned to the hospital. When a prescription called for a controlled drug to be administered, the prison guard staff would fill the syringe with the prescribed dose, and the inmate nurse would then be escorted to the patient who was to receive the medication. When the inmate nurse administered the drug, he would simply pinch a small amount of skin together with his thumb and forefinger and push the needle completely through the patient and into his own thumb or forefinger giving himself the prescribed drug. The nurse would then wipe the area with a sterile cotton ball or place a band aid over the puncture. They were so good at this that even when the prison guard was watching he did not see what actually happened or that there were two small holes in the skin, one where the needle went in, and the other where the needle came out.

Injecting the drug into their hands was not nearly as effective as it world have been if they could have injected it into a vein. I guess the inmates felt this was better than nothing.

The hospital nurses were able to stay high on drugs for nearly two years using this method before someone in the prison staff figured out what was going on.

I can't help but wonder about all the other prisoners that were sick or injured who were in as much or more pain than I who never received any medication to alleviate their pain. Those bastards in the hospital took it all. It seems like everyone who is in jail is running some kind of scam or playing some angle.

CADILLAC ROW

Today public tours of the state penitentiary are not permitted, but they were a popular tourist attraction during the 1950's and 1960's. Guided tours were available every hour from 10:00 to 3:00. Tours were more frequent on the weekends. On a busy weekend there could be up to 6 tours with as many as 10 – 20 visitors on each tour. The charge was fifty cents for adults, and free to children. The money collected from tours went toward the purchase of equipment for the prison sports program and ball teams.

The only individual cells that visitors were allowed to see up close were along one side of the bottom tier of cell house one. The walkway along this one bank of ground floor cells was twenty feet wide and would accommodate large groups. This section of the cell house was known as "Cadillac row."

The only inmates assigned to the elite area were "model prisoners." There was a list of prerequisites: no record of violence, no sexual offenses, no facial hair or excess fat, and no physical handicaps. Above all, you had to keep your cell neat and clean at all times. Floors had to be wiped down each morning after breakfast. Beds had to be made military style with a neat tuck and a very tight blanket.

I did not want to become a public spectacle, but I also did not want to live in the tiny dingy cell in cell house six. I decided to accept the offer and was assigned to cell number eleven about midway down the tier on "Cadillac row" in cell house one.

The idea of having strangers look at me like an animal in the zoo was repulsive, but I was away from my cell at my job assignment during the week, and on the weekends I had the option of going to the yard or to the movie on Sunday. Otherwise, I could be busy reading or writing letters in my cell and perhaps I would not notice all the gawkers.

There was a yellow line two inches wide painted on the floor three feet from the cells all the way down this corridor where the visitors came in. The visitors were told to stay back and not to cross the yellow line. I think it was mostly for dramatic effect. I would often hear the guard that was giving the tour instruct the visitors not to cross the yellow line because these were very dangerous convicted criminals who were capable of striking out at any time.

The inmate in the first cell was designated the tier runner. His cell door was open, and when a tour approached the cell house, his job was to run along the line and announce "visitors – visitors – visitors." This was done to alert the inmates so they were not caught using the toilet during the tour.

One lovely Sunday afternoon I was reading the newspaper as a large tour was being shown through the cell house. All of a sudden the quite whispers of the tour group were shattered by the loud screaming of children as they climbed up the bars of my cell hollering, "Mommy, Mommy, look, there's that man that used to call us "squids."

It was Fat Shirley with a passel of little squids. I was totally embarrassed. I was hollering, "Get down, get away." Mom and the guard were picking the "squids" off the bars and putting them back behind the line. As soon as they pick one off, another one climbed back up the bars. Finally things got under control and the tour group moved on.

JUNK WORKERS

One of the main attractions for the tour groups visiting the state penitentiary was the curio shop. This was a nice little store next to the library where items made by inmates were offered for sale. Many of the visitors came only to purchase items from the curio shop. Some came on a regular basis to buy items to be used as gifts.

Some inmates spent much of their time making items they hoped to sell. These inmates were referred to as "junk workers." Indeed a lot of the stuff was little more than junk. However, much of it was exceptionally nice and very well done. The most popular items were wood, leather and jewelry. The wood workers produced hand-made items such as jewelry boxes, lamps, covered wagons and toys. Some of the leather workers produced beautiful hand-tooled leather products such as belts, billfolds and purses. The jewelry workers bought stones and soft metals, usually copper, from the outside and made bracelets, necklaces, and earrings. There were also inmate artists who did paintings in oil or charcoal.

In order to be a "junk worker," an inmate first had to apply to the cell house commander for a "junk permit" along with a proposal of what he wanted to make and what tools and materials would be needed. Everything produced had to be made by hand; for obvious reasons, power tools of any kind were not permitted.

The difficulty in being a "junk worker" and producing any type of product was accessing material and tools. Everything had to be ordered by mail accompanied by a money order that was issued and approved by the prison finance clerk. The prison staff in the mail room carefully inspected each order when it arrived for any unauthorized items or contraband.

The skills of the "junk workers" were shared with other inmates making similar products and passed along to new workers. Some of the inmates found they had hidden talents that had not previously been explored. They created items of remarkable quality and beauty, so much so that they had difficulty keeping up with the demand. A few of the "junk workers" were real entrepreneurs. They banded together to make cedar jewelry boxes. One would cut the wood to all the right sizes. Another would assemble the parts and make drawers. Another inmate down the tier in his cell would sand and polish. They bought beautiful lush scrap cloth from a casket company to use as lining on the inside. The jewelry boxes they produced were magnificent. They worked hard to meet the demand. They did well and made a lot of money.

I've always thought it was interesting that people could get themselves so far out of line with society that they had to be put in prison. And then, once in prison they became good workers and very productive.

By the spring of 1967, I had been in prison over a year. I met the classification board for my annual review. It was decided that I was a "minimum risk" prisoner. This meant I was eligible to be transferred from the main prison to one of the outside facilities. I was going to leave cell house one, Cadillac row and Mr. Urie all behind.

I was ecstatic. My girlfriend could visit me in an open area. I could walk the ground and not see bars or armed guards. It was almost like being a free man. Being able to see the sunset and hear the birds and smell the grass are blessings that we often don't realize are there. We forget how important the everyday parts of our world are that make it worth everything. Once again I considered myself lucky in being allowed to transfer out of the main institution. I was assigned to the prison dairy.

THE DAIRY

They were black and white. They were Holsteins. They were everywhere. There must have been two or three hundred of them. I knew nothing about cows. I was a city boy. I grew up in Denver. I'm a product of the Denver Public School system. Many folks think if you grew up in Colorado you must be a cowboy. It ain't so. My knowledge of cows was limited to knowing that cows produced milk.

My first observation was that cows are somewhat ill built. I have seen cats and dogs that had litters and at feeding time the babies all lined in a row to nurse. Cows, on the other hand, have four nipples that are only inches apart, and all the nipples are on one teat. It seemed to me that if a cow had three or four babies there was not going to be enough room at the dinner table at feeding time.

Over the next couple of years, I learned a whole lot about cows. It's not a teat; it's an udder. Cows usually only have one calf. Twins are about as common in cows as they are in humans. The gestation period for a cow is about the same as a human: nine months, give or take a few days. A few days after a cow freshens, which means to give birth and come into milk, the calf is taken away from the mother with little or no time for bonding. The calf is taught to nurse at a bucket from a rubber glove. A few days of this and the calf learns to eat from the bucket. The bull calves and some of the heifer calves were taken to town and sold at auction. Many of the heifer calves would be kept if they had good lineage and came from a line of good milk producers.

Holstein heifers can be bred at 13 months of age when they weigh about 800 pounds. It is desirable to have Holstein females calve for the first time between 23 and 26 months of age. While some cows may live considerably longer, the average productive life of a Holstein is only about 3 to 4 years.

A cow that has just given birth can be milked three times a day. In a couple of months, the ability of the cow to produce milk starts to diminish and the cow is moved to the two timer list. This means that it is no longer productive to milk the cow more than twice a day. Finally the cow is only milked once a day. At this point it's necessary to breed the cow again so that she can freshen and start the process over again. Without a calf, the cow will dry up and have no milk to give.

A cow comes into heat much like a bitch dog. There is a discharge that has a scent associated with it that makes cows want to do the nasty. It's called the estrus cycle. During this period, some of the cows in the herd will try to mount the cow in heat. The cows that try to act like bulls and mount the other cows are called "bullers." When we identified a cow that was a prolific buller, she was fitted with a leather harness around her neck that held a large piece of blue chalk. When the "buller" jumped up on the cow in heat, it left a blue stripe on the cow's back. When we saw a cow that had a bunch of blue strips on her back, we knew that it was time to take that cow to see the bull. We had five bulls. The bulls had no season or cycle. They were always ready to do their job.

I was assigned to be the dairy clerk. There were only forty inmates assigned to the dairy. My duties included typing reports and keeping careful records on each cow. Each cow wore a chain around its neck with a large plastic tag with a number on it. To prevent inbreeding, caution had to be used to not send a cow to a bull that might be her father or grandfather. All of the cows at the dairy were registered with the Holstein-Friesian Association of America.

Because I had first aid training as a police officer, I was also the dairy nurse. I was responsible for handing out medications and treating small cuts and abrasions. Occasionally an inmate would come to me with a more serious medical problem than I was able to treat. Being sent to the hospital for medical attention meant going back inside the main prison; most of the inmates dreaded going back inside the walls.

I did most of the paperwork for the other inmates assigned to the dairy, including handing out the mail. It was not bad duty. I kept very busy which made the time pass quickly. I must have been doing something right because after only a few months, I was transferred to the Honor Farm at Pueblo.

THE HONOR FARM

Pueblo is about 20 miles east of Canon City. The Honor Farm was also a dairy farm, but it was bigger than the dairy near the prison at Canon City. My duties at the Honor Farm would remain the same, clerk/nurse, as they had been at the dairy.

There were more cows to keep track of and twice as many inmates, but there were also more freedoms and privileges at the Honor Farm. We had a nice little park for our visits where inmates could walk hand-in-hand with someone special.

Friends and relatives who came to visit could bring a wide variety of gifts that were not permitted at the main prison or medium security. The guard on duty would look through items before they were turned over to the inmate. We were allowed books, magazines, (no adult material) underwear, socks, games, small tools, specialty food items, cigarettes, candy and baked goods. One item that was not permitted was footwear. Inmates were not allowed to have any shoes or slippers that did not have heels. Shoes or slippers with heels had to be sent to the main prison to the shoe shop to have the heels notched before they were turned over to an inmate. The notch was for tracking in the event someone escaped or decided to walk away. Every shoe worn by any inmate in the department of corrections had notched heels. When it was time for an inmate to be released, the shoes he was issued, or any shoes he owned and wanted to take home had new regular heels put on them.

shoe with a notched heel

The meals at the Honor Farm were great. Some of the cooks were better than others, but for the most part they were good at what they did. They were not bound to follow a certain menu as they were inside the walls. The cooks could be a little more creative and could prepare a variety of foods. As a result, many of the meals were specialty dishes and very good. I remember one cook that made the best navy bean soup I have ever tasted. However, barbeque or pizza were never offered. We were served bacon on a regular basis, but there was never any ham. I don't know who got the hams, but the inmates used to joke that the pigs around there must be two inches wide and very long because they only had bacon, no ham.

There were three or four inmates to each large room in the dorm and we all carried our own key to the room we were assigned. We played baseball and touch football. We made and flew our own kites. When the weather was too cold for outside fun, we played poker and pinochle. The Arkansas River was the boundary line for the Honor Farm, and was considered off-limits, but there were a few times during the heat of summer when we frolicked in the boundary line.

Before being sent to the Honor Farm inmates were carefully screened. However, the temptations of more freedom and less security proved to be more than some inmates could handle.

During the two years I was at the Honor Farm there were several unfortunate incidents involving my fellow inmates. One inmate made and sold home brew to the other inmates for several months before he was busted. He used one gallon glass jars to brew hooch in the loft above the barn. During the summer months he used fresh fruit like apples, plums and cherries, which made the best tasting home brew. During the winter months he stole cracked corn that was used in the cow mash from the feed room. He got yeast and sugar from the inmate cook by bribing him with cigarettes. One of his customers was found passed out drunk in the bathroom and later confessed that his booze supplier lived at the end of the hall. They were both sent back to the main prison.

The count at the Honor Farm went down again a few months later when an inmate was stabbed in the neck with an awl, a tool used in leather work, because he didn't or couldn't pay his debts from a poker game.

One summer weekend, the shortstop and one of the out-fielders of our baseball team waded across the river and went to town to get booze. We all hoped they had a good time, because Monday morning they were both back behind the walls in Canon City.

Mary and Clif Karstedt, the people who owned the Avenue Flower Shop where I had worked, drove down to the Honor Farm to visit me on Sunday, September 14, 1969.

It was my 34th birthday. They brought all kinds of baked goods and candy. They even brought Tina, their little Norwich terrier. I remember their visit as if it were yesterday.

When the visit was over and it was time for them to leave, I stood at the edge of the parking area and watched as their car disappeared in the distance. I stood motionless for a long time. Many emotions ran through my head, but one feeling stayed in my mind. I had another moment of truth. I had friends that believed in me. Friends that looked at me with a genuine smile. It was time to make a conscious decision to turn my life around. No one could do this for me; I had to do it myself. The only hand I could count on for help was on my wrist. I was still young. I could make a worthwhile contribution. I could be an honest person with everyone including myself. I had less than a year to serve. Ten months and 25 days to be exact. I would use the time wisely. I made a promise to myself. I vowed to be a success at whatever I did in spite of all the wrong and heartache I had caused. I would do my best to make it right. It is easy to make promises to yourself when you are in jail and there are limited temptations and most decisions are made for you.

I managed to do well and stay out of trouble. The remaining months of my sentence were served at the Honor Farm.

GOING BEFORE THE BOARD

Early in the year I was scheduled to meet the parole board. I knew the parole board looked at three things when considering an inmate for parole.

First, an inmate needed to have a place to stay, preferably with a family member.

Second, an inmate needed a job. Sometimes plans for school were considered in place of employment. Third, an inmate needed to have some money. A few inmates received checks on a regular basis for disability or had some other form of income. The majority of inmates had little or no money on the books. Occasionally an inmate would have someone make a substantial deposit, a few hundred dollars, into his account a few weeks prior to meeting the parole board to make their financial situation look good.

Each inmate was asked to submit a "parole plan" which outlined their intentions for parole. A parole plan had to include at least one of these three stipulations and preferably all three. Most inmates did not manage to meet all the criteria, but were able to show a reasonable parole plan. Each case was given consideration on an individual basis.

Trying to procure employment while still in prison was a challenge. Finding someone to promise a job two or three months down the road was very difficult. All mail leaving the institution contained the penitentiary letterhead. Even before you wrote anything on the paper, a prospective employer knew where you are coming from. Most inmates had their family or friends find some promise of employment for them.

Of course the parole department that had jurisdiction in the area where you planned to live had to accept the inmate as a parolee. This was not usually a problem unless a person wanted to return to an area where he had committed a particularly brutal or heinous crime. This could cause a public outcry from the police or citizens in the community. It was also more difficult to obtain a parole if an inmate wanted to parole out of state.

I went before the parole board armed with a letter from Mary and Clif Karstedt that promised a job at the flower shop upon my release and also offered a place for me to stay in their home. Along with this letter and a good prison record, my parole was a slam-dunk. I was going home.

The atmosphere around other inmates seems to change somewhat after a parole is granted. Some inmates show signs of resentment or envy. They say things like: "You're lucky, man." But, it's hard for them to be supportive when you are the one going home and they are not.

When your time is down to less than a year, you are considered "short." It is a relative term, however, because to a guy doing life, three or four years might seem "short." When inmates get short, they like to boast about how short they are. When an inmate has less than a few weeks left of his sentence, he might say something like: "I'm so short you can hardly see me." Or "I'm so short I could sleep in a match box." Inmates were released in the morning. If an inmate was scheduled to be released on Thursday morning for instance, on Monday morning he would brag that he only had "three days and a get-up." The next morning, he would say, "I've only got two and a get-up."

On Wednesday, April 1, 1970, (April Fools Day) I was transferred to the Pre-Parole Release Center. I spent the next five and a half weeks there. My parole date was Saturday, May 9, 1970.

The Pre-Parole Release Center was a nice place and a great idea. It was located a few miles outside of Canon City. From the road it looked like a well kept motel. There were flowers and shade trees surrounded by a beautifully manicured lawn. Inside the tile floors were waxed and buffed to a high gloss. There was a dining area, a library, a large family room with upholstered furniture, and two or three classrooms. There were about forty individual rooms, and each inmate had his own key.

Not all inmates were eligible for the Pre-Parole Center. If you had been through the program before on a previous sentence, you could not go again. If you were being discharged without parole, you did not go. It could have been beneficial to anyone leaving prison, but space was an issue. There was just not room for everyone who was being released to take advantage of the program.

On my first sentence, I did not go to the Pre-Parole Center. My sentence was commuted to "time served" and I was released immediately.

The goal of the Pre-Parole Release Center was to offer some training in how to cope with everyday situations in a free society. There were lessons in how to order a meal in a restaurant and which piece of silverware to use when eating. Classes were given in how to interview for a job. A lady came once a week to offer advice on dating, and how to treat a lady. The program attempted to cover all the basics needed to function on the "outside."

Many of my fellow inmates were never taught good manners. They had never been exposed to proper etiquette. For them, the program was very helpful and enlightening. I had a good time going to the classes and observing how awkward some of the inmates were. The pre-parole experience was great for the other guy, but I thought I knew it all. I could walk the walk and talk the talk. I would soon discover there were a few things that I was not quite prepared for.

Friday, May 8th 1970, arrived. It was my last full day at the Pre-Parole Center. I did not sleep well that night. I lay in my bed with a million thoughts running through my mind. I looked at my watch, which did not seem to be working, a hundred times during the night. Finally the shadows began to fade and the light of a new day brought hope for a new beginning. I was going home on the bus. My friends Mary and Clif Karstedt and even my girlfriend Thais, who worked there when she was not teaching school, were all needed at the flower shop. It was the day before Mother's Day, one of the busiest days of the year in the flower business. It would have been nearly impossible for any one of them to make the two hour drive to come for me.

FREEDOM

THE BUS RIDE HOME

I could hardly believe that Saturday, May 9th was here. It was a bit unusual, but I was the only inmate being taken downtown to the Greyhound bus station that morning. There was another inmate being released the same day, but his family had come for him in a car, and he was released at 6:00 in the morning.

I thought the two guards who were sent to take me to the bus station seemed to take their own sweet time at coming to pick me up at the Pre-Parole Release Center. When the green station wagon finally arrived, it was after eight. The bus that would take me to Denver was scheduled to board at 9:15 a.m.

I was anxious. My breathing was deep and hard. I tried to act cool as the guards went about getting the paperwork and other stuff done that was necessary for my release. It almost seemed like they were in slow motion. It was all in a day's work for them and they went about it with such routine as to look bored. How were they to know it was the day I had been waiting for forever.

I felt numb during the fifteen minute ride into Canon City. When the state vehicle stopped on the corner in front of the bus station, one of the guards said, "This is it. Keep your nose clean. We don't want to see you back here." "Thanks," I said, and got out. I had everything I owned in a cheap blue plastic suitcase with a leather strap around it to keep it closed. I was 35 years old, and my hair had turned gray. All of the meager belongings in that suitcase have been lost over the years, but I still have a full head of hair, even though it is as white as snow.

The numbness did not go away. I soon realized that every single person knew exactly who I was. They didn't know my name, but they knew I had just jumped out of the joint. I felt as if I stood out and that everyone was looking at me. I probably was not as conspicuous as I thought I was, but I did not look at anyone. During the long bus ride to Denver, I felt people looking at me. I felt ashamed and wished I was wearing something other than the prison issued clothing that I had on.

I'll never forget the strange feelings I had that beautiful Saturday when I got off of the bus in downtown Denver. There was some kind of a protest gathering that had to do with the Kent State University shootings in Ohio earlier that week.

There were beautiful girls wearing very short skirts every-where. I felt out of place and that I should not look at them. It made me very nervous. Many of the girls were with young men and walking with their arms around each other. I saw some of them kiss and it made me feel uncomfortable, like I was seeing something that I had no right to look at. I was so paranoid about the clothes I had on that I went into a store and bought a bright colored windbreaker and discarded the prison jacket I was wearing.

I took a bus from downtown to near where the flower shop was located, and walked the two blocks to 4th and Downing. Everyone in the flower shop greeted me with a big hug, but they were all busy filling orders and arranging flowers. I had a cup of coffee and stood around until Mary thought I needed to be doing something and sent me off with a list and some money to do some shopping at the local Safeway store.

It sounded like fun. It made me feel important and useful. One of the items on the list was oranges. I had no trouble picking out the oranges, but I could not find a bag to put them in. I remembered slots with paper bags in them, but there were none. If something like that were to happen to me today, I would simply find someone to ask where they kept the bags. I was again paranoid. I was afraid they might say something like, "Where the hell have you been?" I just walked around the produce section with all the oranges in my arms trying to act nonchalant waiting to see what other people did with the things they picked out. Pretty soon I saw a lady reach up high, pull a clear plastic bag from a big roll, and rip one off.

I thought when I came home I would be "Mister Cool." Things were not going as I had planned. Things seemed strange; I felt unsure. I had only been out of circulation three or four years. Had things changed that much, or had I just lost my self-confidence?

I had only been home a few days and was still having feelings of uncertainty when my friends Mary and Clif thought it would be nice for me to go get their car washed. They said there was a fancy new car wash just down the street.

All of the car washes I had previously seen were ones where your car was pulled through a series of brushes and soap, and you watched it all from the side through a big window. This was not like that. I was directed to roll up the windows and put the antenna down and drive the car into an area until a red light said, "stop." That was about the time when all hell broke loose. The car started to shake and pitch. The windows were covered with suds and I could not see out. There was a big black thing going around and around like it was trying to get in. The car shook back and forth. I'm not one to panic, but all I wanted was out! I wanted to kick the windows out of that damn car and make a run for it. I had no idea what was going on. Had I watched a car go into the wash area before it was my turn, I probably would have been OK with all this. Even now I remember that day when I go to the car wash. I recently went through a car wash like that for the first time with my little dog Buck, and he was totally freaked. I held him close and told him I understood and that everything would be fine. Buck was not convinced.

ADJUSTING

When I went to see Mr. Heggie, my parole officer, I told him I was having a problem adjusting. I told him I just didn't feel like I fit in. Mr. Heggie set up an appointment for me to talk with Margaret, a state psychologist.

Margaret was willing to listen, but I don't think she knew exactly what to say. I asked her about how people adjust that had been locked up 15 or 20 years. "Oh, they all adjust, it just takes time," she said. "Bullshit," I thought to myself. Anyone released after doing that much time would not make it on the outside without an enormous amount of support or a family who was willing to help them along every step of the way.

I had the feeling that she didn't know anything about how I felt. She was providing lip service to justify her job and patronizing me in an attempt to make me feel better. I only talked with Margaret about thirty minutes. She decided I needed to go to "group."

My group met on Monday and Friday in the evening. By now I had decided that I was doing better, but I felt I had to go to group to pacify Mr. Heggie, my parole officer, who of course was monitoring my progress.

There were eight people in my group. I was the only ex-con. The other patients were sick. After my third session with the group, I quit. I was able to cope better each day, and I felt guilty about taking a place in the group that someone else needed more than I. One girl in my group could only talk about having God help her find her mother so she could kill her. A young man in my group had attempted suicide several times and thought everyone who wore a suit and tie was out to do something bad to him.

I called Mr. Heggie, my parole officer, the next day and informed him that I had left the therapy "group." I assured him that I was adjusting much better and felt the 'group' was more depressing than beneficial. I assured him I was doing well and he need not worry about me. The truth of the matter is that after you've been home for a while, had a few beers, and gotten laid a few times the world seemed like a better place.

Shortly after coming home from jail I learned a lovely lesson from a long-legged lady. She taught me that what you miss the most, you get caught up on the quickest. I still have a vision of her slim silhouette in the early morning light walking across the parking lot of the motel toward her car. She

255

looked so beautiful, but I didn't have the strength to go after her.

FINDING A JOB

Although I wanted desperately to become a productive member of the community and lose the image of "ex-con," there were several setbacks and personal disappointments.

After working at the flower shop for more than a year, I decided to move on. My job there helping out with whatever needed to be done and managing the deliveries was fine and had served me well, but it was not what I wanted to do forever. I told my friends Mary and Clif at the flower shop that I was looking around for more challenge and more money. They were understanding and very supportive.

I soon discovered it was not easy. The job market in the Denver area was good, but not many places were willing to hire a convicted felon.

I found a job as a mechanic's helper for the FBO (Fixed Base Operator) at a small airport east of Denver. I started taking flying lessons on a pay-as-you-go basis. When I had some extra money and could afford to rent an airplane for an hour and pay for an instructor, off we'd go. I got a first class medical certificate and a student pilot certificate. I took my first solo flight at Sky Ranch airport in a Cessna 150 on Tuesday, February 29, 1972. Before long I earned a private pilot license.

After working at the airport for a year, my interest in aviation led to a job working on the line, servicing and fueling much larger aircraft for Combs Gates at Stapleton International Airport in Denver. This was the best job I'd had since the police department. It was interesting, paid pretty well and had some benefits. However, I still spent a lot of my time in bars and chasing women.

During this time, Sandy came into my life. She did great things for my ego. Sandy was much younger than I and was totally fascinated by my bad boy image. She was going to fix everything that was wrong with me. It did not work. We had a whirlwind wedding in a drunken stupor. I did not love her, and I treated her badly. The marriage was doomed from the start, and I did nothing to help make it work. We were divorced after little more than a year.

I worked for Combs Gates for four years, but my drinking, being late for work and being hung-over finally led to my being fired. I had no one to blame but myself. I screwed up big time. I was sick with myself and ashamed to tell my friends that I had been fired from such a neat job.

I worked at some odd jobs for a few months when in April of 1977, another real opportunity came my way. There was an opening for a mechanic at the main warehouse for King Soopers. (A Kroger Company grocery retailer) I had the mechanical skills needed for the position they wanted filled. The job paid union wage and had a great benefit package. I went to their employment office to fill out an application. As expected, the question "Have you ever been convicted of a felony?" appeared on the application. I elected not to respond to the question. I left it blank. I had been turned down so many times before, I felt my chances were better if I had the opportunity to explain the situation face-to-face in an interview.

I received a call just a day or two after filling out the application and was informed that I was the top candidate for the job. I was elated. The man on the phone wanted to know how soon I could start. It was decided that I would report for work the following Monday morning.

I reported as directed and was assigned to a man named Jack who would show me around the work area and tell me what I would be expected to do. Jack and I hit it off right away. This was a dream job. At the end of the first day I hurried to the flower shop to share the good news with my friends Mary and Clif. They were glad for me. We all hugged; it was a happy time.

Tuesday afternoon, my second day on the job, a man came for me and asked that I go with him to the office. In the office a security man for the company told me I was being terminated immediately. They had done a background check and found that I was a convicted felon and that I had failed to mention it on my application. I tried to reason with the man, but he was not interested.

"We're sorry, Art, it's company policy."

As I drove home in my old Volkswagen bug, I had tears in my eyes. I felt sorry for myself. I was so discouraged. I silently asked myself: "What did I do wrong?" "Why is this so hard?" "No wonder the rate of recidivism is so high." "Who will give me a chance?"

THE CACA FACTORY

I had been out of work for a couple of weeks when I heard that they needed entry level workers to train as operators at the Englewood/Littleton Wastewater Treatment Plant.

The cities of Englewood and Littleton are suburbs south of Denver. The treatment facility was built as a joint effort by the two cities for economic reasons. All of the sewage from both cities went to this plant, but it was operated by the city of Englewood, and all of the employees were employees of the city of Englewood.

The thought of working in a wastewater plant did not appeal to me, but I was broke and I needed a job.

When I went to apply, I took the application into the supervisor's office and told him of my record.

"I don't want to waste your time and mine by filling this out if I will not be considered for the job."

"I appreciate your honesty. I don't believe there will be a problem with your past."

I was hired and started on the night shift the next day. The chief operator took me on a tour of the plant. He explained that it was an activated sludge plant, and that the effluent was discharged into the South Platte River. I knew nothing about wastewater treatment other than it smelled really bad.

One of the first jobs I was given was nearly my last. Bob Hitchcock, the chief operator, took me to the basement of the digester building. There were two large pumps that circulated the "stuff" in this huge digester. One of the pumps had become clogged. I was shown how to isolate the pump and lock it out (turn it off) and how to remove the clean-out cover plate. Next I was given two five gallon plastic buckets and instructed to reach into the volute and pull everything out that was wrapped around the impeller and then deposit it all in the buckets.

Wow, it was awful. I think I was given that job as some kind of a test. Perhaps it was some kind of initiation for the job. It is hard to describe what a dirty, slimy and stinking job that was. I thought to myself: "Do I really want this job?" "Should I just walk away and say, "no thanks"? I turned and looked over my shoulder at the chief operator standing behind me. He smiled and said, "It might look like shit to you, but it's bread and butter to me!"

I made it through the shift, and the next night when I reported for work I went directly to the chief operator, Mr. Hitchcock, and said, "If that pump gives you any trouble just let me know." I had made my decision. I was going to stick it out.

At that time, the City of Englewood had a policy whereby if you took any college level courses that made you a more marketable employee in your field, they would pay the tuition.

As soon as I was eligible, I signed up to take classes in water/wastewater at the local community college. I continued to work nights and to attend school during the day.

In Colorado, as in most states, the people that treat water and wastewater are licensed by the state.

I continued to work at the caca factory and go to school for the next three years. My goal was to earn an associate degree in wastewater and pass the state certification board exam and get a class "A" operator's license.

I managed to keep the job and do pretty well in school but there were still frequent bouts with the bottle and periods of time that I was out of control. The first weekend in September of 1980 (Labor Day weekend) was my grand finale. I had the weekend off and started to party on Friday evening. I continued to drink all day Saturday and Sunday. Monday, Labor Day, I was in bad shape. I had spent the night passed out in my car. I had thrown up in my car and on myself. Somehow, even in my drunken/hung-over hell, I realized that I had to do something. I was truly sick and tired of being sick and tired. I made a decision that affected the rest of my life. I decided to stop drinking and smoking.

It occurred to me that if I lived another two weeks, I would be 45 years old. My father literally drank himself to death and died a miserable death at age 57. I felt my life depended on my making a drastic change.

Several other recent memories were beginning to weigh heavy on my conscience. I had a good friend whose opinion I respected. We hung out together and drank together. One afternoon he told me that I was a nice guy, but that I drank too much and that I was not a fun person when I had too much to drink. I shrugged it off at the time, but it remained in my mind. Another incident that haunted me was that I had been at my younger brother's house drinking and shooting pool a few months earlier. My brother Dave is one year younger than I. There was a picture of our father on the wall taken within a year of his death. I pointed to the photo and said to my brother, "The old man looks pretty rough in this one."

"Yeah, you're going to look just like that pretty soon." Dave said.

The message was finally getting through to my soggy brain. I thought to myself that I was not as well off as I had been when I was in prison. I was near the very bottom. At this point my future looked very bleak. I had to stop, or face certain death.

My decision to stop drinking also meant I had to stop smoking. It seemed to me the two were synonymous. If I had a beer in one hand I needed a cigarette in the other. If I were going to quit one, I would also need to quit the other.

The doctors and the therapists who treat addiction claim that a person's state of mind is important in giving up an addiction. Before a person can become free of a dependency on drugs, tobacco, liquor or other substance, that person must really want to quit and also believe he can. Unless an addict truly believes in his heart that he wants to quit, he will usually not be successful. I realized that the only hand that could really help me was on my wrist.

I was ready. I wanted to quit. I had only been fooling myself. Living life in a stupor, trying to scheme a way to get from one drink to the next, is no life at all. The deception and treachery I played out against myself and friends just to drink was taking nearly all my time and energy. I was tired.

My decision was final and immediate. I was not going to *try* to quit, I was going to quit.

GETTING IT RIGHT

ASPEN TREES

The palette that Mother Nature uses to paint Colorado in September has the brightest and most brilliant colors of all. It is truly an unforgettable show of magnificent splendor. It seems that each year is better than the last. The air is clean and crisp. Bright white clouds backlight the majestic mountains. Soon it will all be covered in a blanket of white as the snow falls.

It was a beautiful time in my life both inside and out. I did it. I quit. There is something empowering about taking charge. The self satisfaction that comes from making it happen is enormous. I knew I could do it. My determination to be free of any dependency was very strong. The pride and self confidence I gained from quitting made me feel like a king. I was a winner. There are a number of places a person can turn to when he wants to quit. Alcoholics Anonymous and groups to help overcome drug addiction are readily available for anyone that is ready to quit and wants some help or support. My brother Dave, who also had a drinking problem, quit drinking one year after I did. He has remained sober ever since with the help of Alcoholics Anonymous.

I felt good about the fact that I did it on my own. But, how you quit is not as important as that you do. I would urge anyone that wants to quit to seek some help. Support is available to anyone that reaches out. You can put your bad habits away for good. Take charge; a much better life awaits you.

There was a time in my life when if someone would have said that I could never have another drink or cigarette, I would have said that I didn't want to go on. It was that important to me. The more time that passes since I quit the more ridiculous and insane that statement becomes. I was doing the same things as my father. All the things I hated.

A friend, who was a chief operator at Englewood on another shift, resigned and went to work for the City of Aurora. I lived in Aurora, which is a large suburb of Denver. I went to visit him at his new job at the Aurora wastewater treatment plant. I was impressed. It was a smaller plant and was manned around the clock with only six operators. This meant that the operators were involved in all aspects of the treatment process and even did some of the required lab tests for process control and water quality.

The plant was undergoing a complete remodel and was being rebuilt with new modern equipment. The City of Aurora was a pioneer in the reuse of wastewater by using secondary or tertiary treatment. This advanced degree of treatment and filtration made it possible for the water to be approved for use as irrigation on many of the city parks and golf courses.

I was told that when the remodel was complete, they were going to hire another operator. I went right to City Hall to talk to the Superintendent of the Wastewater Department. I told him that I had been to visit the plant and that I would very much like to be considered for the operator's slot when it became available. I was also totally up front with him about my past. I was told to fill out the required application forms and return them the next day to the superintendent's office. When I returned the next day to talk further about the position, I was told that because of the type of discharge permit under which the plant operated, and since often there was only one operator on duty, every operator had to have a class "A" certification.

At that time I had only a "B" license. I had sat for the "A" exam once and failed. After a couple of meetings with the plant supervisor and the director of the wastewater department, I was hired on a trial basis with the stipulation that I would be on probation for six months, and during that time I would get an "A" license.

After all of the trouble and heartache I had brought on myself for such a long time, things were starting to look bright. After being completely sober for one year, I finally got something right. Thais and I were married. She had always been there for me, even after all the crap I had put her through. She never showed any sign of being discouraged. Thais only saw the bright side. I finished school. I got the class 'A' wastewater license. Thais continued to teach math with the Denver Public School system, and I had a very good job with the City of Aurora. The days were happy for me; I could hardly wait for tomorrow.

My life seemed to get a little better each day. I'm sure that my new found sobriety played a big part in getting my life together. Someone once said that age forces a certain amount of wisdom upon us whether we like it or not. For whatever reason, I was on the right path and I knew it.

I had been released from prison ten years before my decision to put a "plug in the jug." When I got out of jail I felt as though I had been given a second chance. It was a new beginning, a time to make things right. Little did I realize that I was in my own prison. Until I gave up alcohol and had the opportunity to see the world with a clear head and a rational mind, I was not free.

I am continually amazed at the personal accomplishments I am able to achieve since I quit drinking. Nothing I have ever done has brought me more self satisfaction and personal happiness.

Things continued to improve. During the next few years everything in my life seemed to be working for the best. It has to get awfully dark before we can see the stars.

I enjoyed my job working at the Aurora wastewater reclamation facility. I liked the people I worked for and the people I worked with. I felt that I had to try a little harder at my job. I always went a bit farther than was necessary because I thought I was coming from a long way back. I never wanted anyone to say, "What do you expect from an ex-con?" It was a good job. I did well.

CHANGING TIMES

In 1986, I was contacted by Professor Walt Copely, who taught in the criminal justice program at Metropolitan State College in Denver. He asked me to address the students in one of his ethics classes. I was honored. This started a long list of appearances I made to talk to classes of students in the criminal justice program. For many years I was a guest speaker two or three times a year.

Criminal justice courses are designed to educate people who are seeking a career or are working in the field of law enforcement or corrections. I continued to be surprised when I went to visit with these students. I started by giving the students some information about the Denver police scandal and my involvement. At the end of my speech, I would ask for questions. They asked some tough questions. I probably learned more from them than they did from me. They were so professional despite their young age. Many of their questions were so thoughtful it brought painful memories: "How did this get started?" "How could you let this happen?" It took some soul searching to try and give an honest answer.

When I was a police officer there were no classes offered in criminal justice. Words like "diplomacy" and "ethics" were not heard. Defusing conflict without someone getting hurt was not part of the agenda.

During the 1980's, most of the classes were comprised of male students. As time went by, I noticed more and more women in the classroom. By the year 2000, the classes were nearly evenly divided between male and female students. I enjoyed my visits to the criminal justice classes. I felt as though I had something to say that might make a difference. This led to my next attempt to be a useful citizen and make a contribution to the community.

The 18th judicial district in Colorado was soliciting members of the community to serve as volunteer probation officers. They asked for adults who could work a minimum of 10 hours a week who had an interest or some knowledge in dealing with offenders. I volunteered. There was a little red tape because of my past, but I was accepted into the program and began training classes held each Saturday for a month. In February, 1991, I became a volunteer probation officer.

(Just for your information, probation is what you are given instead of jail time. Parole is usually what you are on after being incarcerated.)

The cases assigned to the volunteers were considered to be less serious than some or were cases of young offenders who were in trouble for the first time. It was interesting work.

Some of the excuses I heard as a probation officer were the same ones I had invented 25 years ago.

I spent as much time as I could counseling each of my clients. I hoped that I got through to at least some of them.

I had been assigned several cases from one of the regular probation officers because they were doing well and nearing the end of their probation sentence. The regular probation officer was a large woman named Helen. She was a no non-sense lady that was considered very tough. Because she was very stern with her clients, Helen had earned the nickname "Big Hell."

Shortly after I started, Helen left the 18th judicial district to work in another district. In reading her case notes about the clients I had been assigned, I noticed something that puzzled me. Helen kept extensive notes and quite often when she wrote what a client had to say in response to her questions she world draw brackets around their reply and mark in the margin LLPF. I saw this a lot, but only in the cases I had from Helen. I asked some of the other probation officer about the significance of LLPF. None of them had a clue.

Several months later there was a regional seminar for proba-tion officers and I was lucky enough to be able to attend. I was having a cup of coffee and eating my cookie when lo and behold I saw "Big Hell." I got Helen aside and asked her about her notes. What did LLPF mean when written beside clients' responses?

She laughed and said, "Oh, that stands for 'Liar, liar pants on fire'."

BACK TO PRISON

One morning when I reported for my day at the probation department I saw a notice on the bulletin board that said any of the probation officers who would be interested in a bus trip down to Canon City to tour the state penitentiary to sign up in the main office. I could hardly wait. When the day came for the trip, there were seventeen of us signed up for the tour. We boarded the bus at 8:00 am for the two hour ride to the big house. We were even going to be treated to lunch in the prison dining hall.

The people in charge of the probation department were aware of my background and prison record. However, the regular probation officers and other volunteers who I worked with were not. I did not volunteer the information.

When the bus arrived at the parking lot in front of the prison, I felt a little queasy. I wanted to do this, but suddenly I was not sure it was a good idea. We were all carefully searched and some items like pocket knifes were left with guards at the reception area. We were separated into small groups of about six each to be escorted into the main prison.

There were a series of "locks" to go through. These small areas were set up so that as you walked into one, the door to let you proceed would not open until the door behind you had closed.

I do not suffer from anxiety. I have never panicked. However, about mid-way through the "locks," my breathing quickened. I had a tight feeling in my chest. All of a sudden I thought to myself, "Oh, God, I've been tricked." I nearly lost it. I did not want the others to see the fear in my face. I must have been as white as snow. Someone asked if I were OK?

"Yeah, I'm fine," I lied.

After we got into the courtyard inside the main prison I was able to gain my composure. That place sure gives new meaning to living in a gated community. I think we must have been given the "grand" tour, because we got to see more than I expected. We were even allowed to go inside one of the cell houses.

There were two guards with us acting as tour guides. One of the probation officers asked   something about the prison to one of the guards. The guard politely informed him, "We don't use the word prison anymore; this is a correctional facility." At which time I said, "It looks like a prison to me." (A rose is a rose, and regardless of what they are called, a penitentiary is a nightmare from hell.)

One thing was certain. There had been a great deal of change since I was paroled over twenty years ago. When I was an inmate, unless you were in your own cell or in the shower, you remained fully dressed including wearing a shirt that was buttoned to the second button from the top. Facial hair was not permitted. If your hair was over your ears, one of the screws (guards) would grab you up and march your ass off to the barber shop. Every inmate had a job. Even if you just dusted the bars or moped the tier. None of this is true now.

I could hardly believe what I saw when we went into one of the cell houses. We were kept in a group on the main floor of a large cell house. We could see from one end to the other and also up at the rows of cells that were three tiers high. There were more than twenty cells on each tier. Along the rails of each tier were inmates just hanging around. I thought that a lot of them looked like Charles Manson. Many of the inmates were not wearing shirts. Belts were not allowed and some of their pants were so low, butt cracks were common. Some wore "doo rags" (bandanas) tied around their heads. Others had hair down to their shoulders. I saw some pony tails and even some with braids. Many of the inmates displayed a wide variety of bad skin art. ("Jail house" tattoos.)

I had to use a bit or restraint to keep from tipping my hand. At one point I caught myself just before saying, "Well that's not the way it used to be."

Most of the probation officers thought the tour was very informative. I was a bit disgusted. How could it have come to this? I thought to myself that there must be some middle ground between the chain gangs of years ago and what I saw today.

Lunch was very nice. We had a salad, vegetables and chicken breast. There was white cake with chocolate frosting for dessert. The dining room had been painted and redecorated. It was clean. There were murals on some of the walls. The steam tables for serving food were still there. I looked at them a long time remembering the pain I had felt years before.

The visit to the state penitentiary had been a jolt of reality for me. It took the wind out of my sails. As we rode home on the bus I stared out the window and thought to myself how lucky I was to be on the outside looking in as opposed to the other way around.

I quit my volunteer work with the probation department about a year later. The paperwork was becoming a little overwhelming, and my regular job with the City of Aurora was taking much of my time.

Photograph of Colorado State Penitentiary taken from Sky Line Drive.
July 1991

CRIMINALS

The high crime rate in this country affects all of us. If there were a magic bullet, we would have pulled the trigger long ago.

What is the real problem? Why are some people so bad and other people so good?

The rate of recidivism would indicate that our prison system is not very effective.

Dr. Edward J. Latessa, a nationally known researcher and expert on repeat criminals said,

"You have to target attitudes, values and beliefs. When it comes to stopping repeat criminals, talk therapy focusing on the past doesn't work. Neither do boot camps or drug education programs. Incarceration, as popular as it is, works only half the time.

"An alternative solution: teaching specific behavioral changes that offenders can implement immediately. You have to teach offenders new ways to behave.

"That includes getting offenders into jobs, banning their association with troublesome acquaintances, fostering involvement in sober activities, identifying positive mentors and teaching them how to be assertive rather than passive and how to spot the triggers that lead to illegal behavior. You must target attitudes, values and beliefs." *

* <u>The Denver Post</u>. November 2, 2007

I believe it starts at home when we are very young and our values are first being learned. What we are taught in the beginning as little children determines the way we behave.

No one read to me when I was a little boy. I'm not blaming my parents, they just didn't know better.

When I was a little boy, my parents sent me off to school to learn the three R's. They thought that would be enough. By then I should have been learning a different three R's.

Respect for self.

Respect for others and

Responsibility for all your actions.

Had I been taught and practiced these three lessons in the beginning, I believe I would have made better choices as an adult.

Responsibility simply translates to our ability to respond.

You need a license to go hunting. You need a license to operate a motor vehicle. You need a license to do a lot of things. You do not need a license to have children. No experience needed. Responsibility is not necessary.

After all the time I spent in prison and talking with hundreds of inmates, it is my belief that the majority of the two million people behind bars in this country today were not wanted as children.

ANOMALIES

There are some things associated with the Denver police scandal that I find rather peculiar. I find it curious, for instance, that during the scandal no one from the district attorney's office or any of the special investigators ever questioned any of the wives of any of the police officers involved. Not one wife was ever questioned about anything, even when the grand jury was convened. It was no secret that the wives of many of the safe burglars in the department were aware of their husbands' activities. I know mine was. It would be difficult to be involved in that kind of activity and hide it from your spouse. The wives of the other policeman who I was involved with in safe burglaries were aware of their husbands' involvement and were happy to spend the extra money. The wives who knew were at least guilty of conspiracy and receiving, both of which are felonies. Why were they never questioned? Why were they not threatened with jail time? Why were they not used as leverage?

Another surprising matter was the fact that during all of this burglary mess no one was shot, or committed suicide. I recall occasions when policeman would make threats about what they would do if anyone ever tried to rat them out or squeal on them. I do know of some threats that were made at gunpoint. However, during this long and bitter investigation that involved so many policemen, and got very ugly at times, it's a wonder that no one was ever gunned down. There was one shooting incident. The shooting involved Keith Hutton and a woman named Sally. Keith Hutton was one of the major players in the Denver police scandal. He had been a Denver police officer for several years before his arrest in 1961. Sally was his live-in girl friend (Keith maintained she was only his housekeeper.) A few months after his arrest, they had a violent argument over his involvement in a safe cracking job. During the struggle, Sally was shot in the abdomen with Keith's service revolver. By the time they got her to the emergency room at Denver General Hospital, she claimed the wound was self inflicted. Sally survived the shooting, but we'll never know what really happened.

I also find it very strange that the police scandal never reached any farther than the uniformed division. In 1966, five years after the scandal, Gerald Foster earned a PhD from the University of Southern California in Political Science, Public Administration.

His doctoral thesis was entitled: <u>Police Administration and the Control of Police Criminality: A Case Study Approach</u>. It was an in-depth study of the Denver police scandal. It was revealed in his report that the Denver Police Department had many incidents of corruption going back as far as anyone could remember, at least as far back as the Second

World War. Perhaps police corruption had not reached the heights that it had by the time I was arrested in 1960, but it had been prevalent for a long time. Many police officers were promoted from the ranks of patrolman to detective over the years. With the exception of one detective who had only been promoted to detective a few months before the scandal, no one above the rank of uniformed patrolman was arrested. There was only one uniformed sergeant arrested. I don't believe that it is realistic to think that the scandal did not go deeper and higher up than it did. Were the detectives protecting themselves? Was the opportunity to be a burglar removed when they were promoted? Had the statute of limitations expired?

Something else that is totally out of the norm is the rate of recidivism. It is a well known fact that over half of the people who are incarcerated today have been there before or will return on a new charge. The rate of recidivism in this country is a national disgrace. Many states spend as much money on prisons and the handling of criminals as they do on education.

For many, it seems that once you fall into the system it is a difficult cycle to break. Many prisoners go back to prison time after time. They almost think of it as a home away from home. They are doing life on the installment plan; they just don't realize it. However, out of all the policemen who were sent to prison, I was the only one to be arrested again and to be returned to prison. There must be a key in this. Was it because none of the policemen were in trouble with the law as juveniles? Might it be that the policemen all had at least a high school diploma, and in many cases had been to college?

I also wonder why after all that happened in Denver with the police department that involved so many lives and touched so many people that someone has not written a book or made a movie.

PARDON ME

In the spring of 2000, after nineteen years, I retired from the City of Aurora. Most of the people who knew me at the City of Aurora were aware of my past and over the years my co-workers and other friends in the utility department shared many good laughs over my being an ex-con. It was all in good fun. I was never offended and I often laughed the loudest. This good humor carried over to my retirement party when the boss asked my wife Thais to cut the cake. She had a bit of difficulty. Inside the beautiful cake, my friends had baked a hack saw blade. We all had a big hoot over that.

I was a bit lost after retirement, but soon found plenty of activities to fill my days. I played poker a couple of times a week, went to the gym every other day, rode my bike and played tennis. Thais and I took a nice trip each year. I worked on several home improvement projects around the house and have always been quick to help my neighbors.

By March of 2000, when I was making plans to retire, I decided to make application to Colorado Governor Bill Owens for a pardon. Based on the many positive accomplishments I had made and the worthwhile contribution I was making to the community, I felt I was a good candidate to be given a pardon. It had been thirty years since my release and I had an outstanding record since that time.

There is a list of documents that must be submitted along with forms to be completed when making an application for a pardon. I got everything together along with a letter to the Governor explaining why I should be considered for a pardon. After several weeks, I was notified that my application had been denied.

I was disappointed. I did not feel as bad for myself as I did for the many friends that had written such glowing letters of recommendation on my behalf. My immediate supervisor and other supervisors with the City of Aurora had written some wonderful letters as had some of my neighbors and friends. I had some nice letters from some of the professors of criminal justices classes I had addressed. I had recommendations from the probation department where I had worked as a volunteer.

I had to write them all a note thanking them for their kind letters and support, and telling them I had been turned down for a pardon.

The Governor said that I could apply again in two years. I thought to myself, "Why bother?" A felon is allowed to vote after the completion of their parole. The only thing I could not do as a convicted felon was to own a firearm. Being able to carry a gun was not something I thought I needed to do. It would have been nice to have a pardon for my children's sake, but perhaps that is not important either.

About a year after the Governor had denied my application for pardon, an attorney friend of mine told me that I should not have tried to do this on my own. He said I made a mistake in not hiring an attorney to represent me. He said I should have retained an attorney, preferably one that was on the advisory board for the Governor, and had my case presented to the Governor in a more professional manner by an officer of the court.

I said, "Are you implying that I did not grease the right wheels of the system?"

"That's exactly what I'm saying," he said.

HAPPY TIMES

I take special joy in each day. The days and weeks and months are more precious than they have ever been before. Even though I hate to admit it, I'm in the twilight years of my life. I'm in my seventies now and the shadows are getting long. Not being able to jump as high or run as far as I once could weighs heavy on my heart. Inside every old person is a young person wondering what happened? I could tell young people that this will happen to them sooner than they think, but they would no more listen to me than I would have when I was young.

We all have the same number of hours each day, but we don't all have the same number of days. Learning to manage our time well is as important as managing our money. We need to have realistic goals. We don't have to be first; there is more to life than increasing its speed. Life is not a sprint, it's a marathon.

People are not very self assured. They lack confidence and are generally not as happy as they would like us to believe. Most people believe that others are more confident and happier than they are. We live in a world where being somewhat anxious seems to be normal or accepted. Our newspapers and television news are filled with reports of crime, disaster and generally unpleasant events. We all know people who are turning to therapy or drugs or reaching out for something to help them cope.

In the second paragraph of the Declaration of Independence it states, "That all men are created equal, that they are endowed by their Creator with certain unalienable rights, that among these are Life, Liberty and the *"Pursuit of Happiness."*

I interpret that to mean that we all have the right, and are free to find happiness. There is joy to be found in the work and effort to make your dreams come true. Happiness is not something you can go out and get. Traveling to distant lands seeking happiness is not the answer. It is a by-product of the journey we have on our way.

Unfortunately, some people never find happiness. Others have so much love to give and are so unselfish in their care of others that happiness surrounds them. People that have found happiness are usually easy to spot. It is reflected in their faces, their friends, and their spirit. Happy people are fun to be around; their attitude is contagious.

I asked my wife, Thais, (she's the one who brings happiness to my world) about what makes people happy? She contends that it's all in one's attitude and how they perceive things. She said that one person could be happy in a situation where another person would not be happy in the same situation. She thinks that people see pretty much what they look for, and that they are about as happy as they make their mind up to be.

I have asked many people if they could tell me what it is that makes a person happy. A couple of people told me that most of the people whom they knew that seemed genuinely happy had suffered a tragedy in their past or have overcome a real hardship at one time.

The Dalai Lama said, "Not getting what you want is sometimes a wonderful stroke of luck."

My friend Dave Walcher, who is a Chief with the Jefferson County Sheriff's Department said, "How a person responds to adversity is what makes a champion."

I'm really doing well. Today my life is a great big double scoop of cool happiness. Every day is a diamond; I can hardly wait for tomorrow. Believing I'm happy is all it takes. I'm upbeat and full of enthusiasm. I'm high on life. I want to sing, "I'm at the top of the heap; if my friends could see me now!"

I wish I could pass along a recipe for everyone to follow that would bring instant happiness. Of course we all know that's not going to happen, but I'll give you some hints that I use that might get you pointed in the right direction.

If you don't do something nice for someone every day, you're a loser. Take your dog for a walk. If you don't have a dog of your own, you could find someone in your neighborhood that would be grateful to someone for walking his dog. (If you don't have a dog to love, perhaps you should visit a shelter and get one.) Write a nice note to someone you care about. Call a friend to say you're thinking about them. Tell the people who are close to you that you love them. Do it now.

THE STAR IN MY HEAVEN

The biggest contributor to my happiness is my wife, Thais. She is the foundation of my life. She is the glue that holds my world together. I play poker and occasionally make a wager on the outcome of a sporting event. At one time I subscribed to a news letter about gambling. It was called The Intelligent Gambler. Thais said that was an "oxymoron."

Thais thinks gambling is a waste of time and money. She would never do that. When I met her she had never been married, had a wonderful career as a math teacher with the Denver Public Schools. She was working on her master's degree, had a new car, a lovely apartment and a ton of friends. With all of this going for her, this beautiful lady made the decision to marry a man who is an alcoholic, has been in three failed marriages and has done two sentences in the state penitentiary. And she's says she is not a gambler – yeah, right! What do you suppose her odds were on that one?

Today after twenty seven years I think it would be safe to say that she stepped up to the plate and drove one out of the park. My wife, Thais, is the one that makes my sun shine.

We have a great marriage. We always have a wonderful time when we are together.

I would like to describe what this lady has meant to me for over a quarter of a century, and how much I love her, but words will not be adequate; there are none.

Happiness is not the same unless you can share it. Doing something fun or going somewhere is not nearly as exciting as sharing it with someone you truly care about.

The love and respect that I share with this woman has made me rich beyond belief. I particularly appreciate her loyalty and patience with me. During the early days of our relationship, she followed me down some dark paths where there were no flowers to pick.

Thais is my best friend. We have no secrets. No one knows me better than she does, and no one knows that better than I do. Deception erodes the foundation of marriage. The survival of marriage is based on truth and respect.

Thais 2008

Occasionally Thais is away for the weekend attending agility competition with our two Cairn Terriers. (Toto in the Wizard of Oz is a Cairn Terrier.) I am lost without her, but I take solace in knowing she will soon return.

In closing, let me say it's not what you start in life that's important, it's what you finish. Try again. Failure is no more fatal than success is permanent.

Let the Midnight Special shine its ever-lovin' light on you.

- THE END -

Printed in the United States
144071LV00002B/37/P